At the
LORD'S TABLE

At the
LORD'S TABLE

Communion Prayers
for All Seasons

DOUGLAS B. SKINNER

CHALICE
PRESS
ST. LOUIS, MISSOURI

Cover art: FotoSearch
Cover and interior design: Elizabeth Wright

www.chalicepress.com

Print: 9780827200531   EPUB: 9780827200579   EPDF: 9780827200586

Printed in the United States of America

For all the elders who through the years
have prayed at the Lord's table for me.

Central Christian Church, Pocatello, Idaho (Student 1974-75)
First Christian Church, Melissa, Texas (Student 1976-1979)
Lubbockview Christian Church, Lubbock, Texas (Associate 1979-1980)
First Christian Church, Plainview, Texas (1980-84)
Memorial Drive Christian Church, Houston, Texas (1984-1993)
First Christian Church, Amarillo, Texas (1993-1997)
Northway Christian Church, Dallas, Texas (1997–Present)

Contents

CHAPTER 4
Communion Prayers for the Church Year
41

CHAPTER 5
Communion Prayers for Special Sundays
77

CHAPTER 6
Communion Prayers for Special Occasions
101

Conclusion: Scripting the Moment
111

Appendix: "On Prayer"—Alexander Campbell
115

Sources Cited
117

1

So, You're an Elder

Introduction

It is the question that gets asked every year when the church's nominating committee approaches an individual with the wonderful news that he or she has been recommended for a position of spiritual leadership within the life of a local congregation. When asked to serve as an elder, the inevitable question gets asked: *"So, just exactly what does an elder do?"*

To answer this perennial question of church life, we typically direct people to the appropriate biblical passages and the congregation's relevant organizational documents. There the qualifications and responsibilities of an elder in the church get spelled out in some detail. But I am not naive. I know that there is also an unofficial oral tradition that typically accompanies the church's official answer to the question of what elders do, and it goes something like this: *"Elders pray...Elders pray the communion prayers at the Lord's table on Sunday mornings."* Nominees who have learned how to manage their fear of public speaking usually answer, *"Well, that's easy enough. I can do that. I can pray."* This resource is written with the person in mind who has ever said or thought those words.

The Communion Prayer

An elder is someone who has been recognized by a specific congregation as having a representative degree of spiritual maturity within that community of faith. The office of elder does not require moral perfection or the status of a capital "*S*" Saint, but it does require men and women who are spiritually alive and still growing. It is no accident that men and women who give evidence of a vital prayer life are the ones who are routinely asked to serve as the elders of their congregations—women and men who display the fruit of the Spirit (Gal. 5:22–23), who exhibit a process of being actively conformed to the image of Jesus Christ (Rom. 8:29), and who display the mind of Christ (Phil. 2:5–8). People become elders because they are known to be people who are abiding in Christ (Jn. 15:4), and that does not happen apart from a life of vital prayer. But elders need to know that they will be asked to pray at the Lord's table a special kind of prayer.

The communion prayer is neither a prayer of general intercession nor a prayer of private devotion. The communion prayer is not the right vehicle for the voicing of your own personal hurts and hopes, just as it should not be a substitute for the church's morning prayer or an imitation of the minister's weekly pastoral prayer. God clearly cares about our dreams and fears, and wants to hear all about them. God should certainly be thanked for the beauty and blessings of the day. The needs of the sick, the wounds of the grieving, the fears of the troubled, and the joys of the faithful should all be given prayerful expression in the gathered community of faith—but not at the Lord's table. The communion prayer has a different purpose and a governing content.

In the 1991 *Word to the Church on the Lord's Supper* from the Committee on Theology of the Council on Christian Unity of the Christian Church (Disciples of Christ), these instructions were given in the section entitled "Prayers at the Table" (150):

> The communion prayers…should include as a basic element the offering of thanksgiving. Christians here

express gratitude for God's love, for the life and death of Jesus Christ, and for the gift of salvation...

The prayers at the Table are also to include a petition for the presence of the Holy Spirit, through whose power the bread and wine provide spiritual nourishment for the refreshing of our faith, the upbuilding of the body of Christ, and our living as faithful servants of Jesus Christ in the world...

It is also appropriate in communion prayers to focus on our remembrance of the sacrifice of Jesus Christ, our anticipation of God's ultimate victory, our awareness of the presence of Jesus Christ among us, and our appreciation for the richness of meaning conveyed by the Lord's Supper.

A word of thanksgiving, a petition for the presence of the empowering and enlivening Spirit, a remembrance of the sacrifice of Christ, a nod in the direction of Christian hope and an acknowledgement of the real presence of the Risen Christ—that's a big assignment for a little prayer.

You can easily access some helpful guides to learn more about the constitutive elements of a communion prayer. Thomas Toler's *The Elder at the Lord's Table* (1954) and several of Keith Watkins's books—especially *The Feast of Joy* (1977) and *Celebrate with Thanksgiving* (1991)—are denominational standards worth becoming familiar with as an elder. You will detect the pattern they identify in many of the prayers I have written for this book:

1. A spiritually appropriate naming of God
2. A communal rather than private tone of expression
3. The identification of some particular aspect of the biblical meaning of communion appropriate to the season of the church year or the theme of the day
4. A reference to the institution of the Lord's supper and the event of the crucifixion of Jesus Christ
5. A word of thanksgiving for the benefit of salvation appropriate to the particular meaning of communion earlier identified

6. An invocation of the Holy Spirit's indwelling and empowering presence

Most of these elements of a communion prayer are familiar to us. The one exception is the explicit petition for the presence of the Holy Spirit. Called the *epiclesis* in the history of Christian worship (from the Greek word for "invocation"), this petition is essential in a communion prayer because it is the action of the Holy Spirit that makes the dynamic connection between the outward signs of bread and wine and the inward reality of God's presence, power, and provision in Jesus Christ in our hearts. For the communion service to be more than just a taste of bread and a sip of wine, the Holy Spirit must be involved.

"Brief and Pertinent"

In *The Christian System* (1836), Alexander Campbell, one of our denominational founders, provided a detailed description of the communion service, which, in his judgment, "furnishes the nighest approach to the model which we have in our eye of good order and Christian decency in celebrating this institution." He noted that "the thanksgiving before the breaking of the loaf, and the distributing of the cup, were as brief and pertinent to the occasion, as the thanks usually presented at a common table for the ordinary blessings of God's bounty."

What Alexander Campbell really liked about the communion prayers he heard in that service were that they were *"brief and pertinent."*

Brevity as one of the criteria of a good communion prayer has a clear biblical foundation. Part of the criticism that Jesus had for the public praying of his day was that it was just too long and drawn-out. "When you are praying, do not heap up empty phrases as the Gentiles do;" Jesus said, "for they think that they will be heard because of their many words" (Mt. 6:7). Think of some of the New Testament's most powerful prayers. This sampling is from the gospel of Luke:

> *"Here I am, the servant of the Lord; let it be with me according to your word."* (1:38)

"Master, now you are dismissing your servant in peace, according to your word; / for my eyes have seen your salvation." (2:29–30)

"God, be merciful to me, a sinner!" (18:13b)

"Father, if you are willing, remove this cup from me; yet, not my will but yours be done." (22:42)

"Father, into your hands I commend my spirit!" (23:46)

Clearly, the length of a prayer says nothing about its power. Perhaps the very best prayers are short and frequent, and so brevity is something we value in our prayers at the Lord's table, as is pertinence.

Unfocused communion prayers tend to ramble, and so an elder must understand what he or she stands at the Lord's table to do when it is time to pray over the bread and cup. At the Lord's table an elder never stands alone. Two calls combine in that moment at that place: (1) to carefully represent the gathered community of faith as the designated spiritual leader who has been asked to give voice to their highest aspirations and deepest convictions; and (2) to faithfully "hand on" to that community of faith the rich tradition of Christianity's varied understandings of the meaning of the Lord's supper. This is why James White called communion prayers "prayed theology" (1989, 60). The elder who prays in the awareness of these two calls is most likely to offer a pertinent prayer when he or she presides at the Lord's table.

A third criterion for our communion prayers that can be legitimately derived from Alexander Campbell's observations of the worship service, is the celebration of communion in simplicity of expression. Alexander Campbell preferred plain and unaffected language when praying. I have heard this described as conversational praying. It is prayer without pretense.

A "Disciple" Way of Praying?

This is why simplicity and straightforwardness are hallmarks of the kind of authenticity that we Disciples prize so highly in our spirituality. We like prayers that come from the heart and connect with the spirit. As in most things, we Disciples prefer freedom over form. And at the Lord's table this has meant a real fondness for prayers that are offered spontaneously on the spot rather than ones that are read from a book. It is part of our Reformed theological heritage to be suspicious of set forms of prayer.

Rightly or wrongly, many Disciples believe that extemporaneous praying is less inclined to become the kind of formal, wooden praying that Jesus Christ criticized as "heap[ing] up empty phrases" in his Sermon on the Mount (Mt. 6:7). The average people in the pews of a typical church will tell you that their preference is for spontaneous, heartfelt, Spirit-filled prayers offered simply rather than exactly worded, pre-prepared, and carefully read compositions.

Opposed to both creeds and liturgies as unnecessary and even spiritually illegitimate attempts to standardize Christian faith and practice on the basis of something other than the New Testament, the ideal for communion prayers in our churches is that they be characterized by an engaging simplicity, a personal quality, a biblical faithfulness, and a heartfelt authenticity. So, why bother with this book? Our spiritual heritage would seem to argue persuasively against its existence and use. Well, before throwing it aside, let me make a case for its legitimacy by introducing you to something from our spiritual heritage called "conceived prayer."

An "Acceptable Combination"

Alexander Campbell was troubled by the way that the genuine spirit of Christian devotion could degenerate so quickly into cold formalism, and degrade so easily into lifeless ceremony. He knew that extemporaneous praying could be sloppy, silly, scrambled, self-indulgent, and even spiritually dangerous, especially when it was offered in a representative way at the defining moment of public worship from behind the Lord's table in the communion prayer.

In his 1831 essay "On Prayer" in the *Millennial Harbinger,* Alexander Campbell sought to remedy the most common defects he heard in the public praying of the spiritual leaders of our churches by urging them to spend more time with the prayers found in scripture. He created a lectionary of twenty-two biblical prayers and benedictions, twelve from the Old Testament and ten from the New Testament, which he then encouraged church leaders to use to learn how to pray for themselves. (See the Appendix for the titles of these texts.) This approach to praying was part of Alexander Campbell's Reformed roots.

The Reformed tradition had taught Alexander Campbell three basic ways to approach prayer: (1) Read set prayers from a book, but this could become spiritually inauthentic; (2) pray spontaneously from the heart, but not everyone has the gift to do this intelligently or intelligibly; (3) use book-read prayers and offer spontaneous prayers. The Reformed tradition taught people that there was some important spiritual middle ground. They called it "conceived prayer," and they viewed it as an "acceptable combination" of form and freedom, structure and spontaneity (Watkins 1966, 73).

In conceived prayer, a Christian was taught to "stock" one's heart and head with appropriate thoughts and phrases drawn from scripture and the Christian tradition, which could then be used to construct prayers of one's own. I have heard this approach to praying compared to the girders that are fastened together in the building of a bridge, or the ingredients that are mixed together in the baking of a cake. Conceived prayer takes seriously the concern for content by its habitual reference to scripture, and the concern for vitality and relevance in our praying by pushing that content through the processor of our individual hearts and the life of our communities of faith. The hymn writer Isaac Watts, a big proponent of this kind of praying, described conceived prayer as "clothing the sense of our hearts in fit expressions" (1730). It is one of the best ways for a Christian to grow in his or her capacity for, and expression in, public praying.

How to Use This Resource

Perhaps the best way to think of this resource is as training wheels for your ministry of prayer at the Lord's Table as an elder of the church. Some readers will choose to use prayers from this book verbatim when they go to the Lord's table.

That's a perfectly acceptable option. The assurance I can give
to those of you who will take this approach is that each prayer
you'll find here has been composed from my heart in
response to the deep stirrings of the Word and the Spirit.

I like the story told about Peter Marshall, the chaplain of
the United States Senate from 1947 to 1949. When he was
first asked to serve as the Senate chaplain, he was told that
one of the requirements of the job was to have a copy of the
prayer that he would offer at the opening of each session
turned in before it was actually prayed so that it could be
entered into the Congressional Record. But Peter Marshall
was a "pray-from-the-heart" kind of Christian leader. His
first instinct was to turn down the job offer because he felt
that the requirement of pre-prepared prayers would hinder
the work of the Holy Spirit in and through his heart. Then
one of Peter Marshall's friends pointed out that a pre-
prepared prayer could be just as heartfelt and Spirit-
prompted composed at his desk the night before as it could
be being spontaneously offered on the spot. I trust that these
prayers can be too.

Other readers will turn to this book and flip through it
rather quickly, maybe on the night before they are scheduled
to pray at the Lord's table. More inclined to "pray-from-the-
heart" and "on-the-spot," this reader is only interested in
seeing how somebody else has done it. What I hope this kind
of reader will find in what they read here is a model of
faithfulness that they can then imitate. Hippolytus (c. 170—
c. 236), the church father whose writings provide us with
some of our most important insights into the worship
practices of the early church, noted that "it is not at all necessary to recite the same words" in a communion prayer. He
explained that "in giving thanks to God" at the Lord's table
each elder is free to "pray according to his ability." He added
that every elder in that wonderful freedom was still obliged
to "pray what is sound doctrine" (quoted in White 1990, 229).
The freedom we have as elders in our offering of the communion prayers at the Lord's table is not without restraint. The
control that must be exercised over them is not a control of
word or phrase, but a control of thought and content. I trust

that those who will skim these prayers will detect the *"pattern of sound words"* (2 Tim. 1:13, RSV) that governs what we do at the Lord's table, and find a way to do the same thing in their own way.

Finally, it is my deepest hope that some readers of this book will use it in their own cultivation of the spiritual discipline of conceived prayer. These communion prayers come from a heart that has been well "stocked" with phrases, words, and thoughts from the deep wells of Holy Scripture and Christian tradition. If these prayers can help cut channels in your souls to those pools, I would be most pleased.

2

Communion Prayers Based on Meanings of Communion

A complexity marks the spiritual significance of the Lord's supper in the tradition of the Christian Church (Disciples of Christ). Although engraved on the front of many of the Lord's tables in our churches are the words "Do this in Remembrance of Me," identifying our historic origins in the "memorialist" tradition of Reformed Christianity, we have never been limited as a church to just one understanding of the meaning of communion. Our commitment to "speaking where the Bible speaks" leads us to an appreciation of the diverse ways that the New Testament itself discusses the significance of the broken bread and the shared cup.

If our denominational understanding of the meaning of the Lord's supper were just a single position, then our spiritual task as elders at the Lord's table would be a simple matter of repeating a standard formula. But because our understanding as a church of the meaning of communion is intentionally just as diverse as the biblical witness itself, our theological task as elders is considerably more demanding. We need to be constantly expanding the ways that our congregations understand and appreciate the significance of the Lord's supper by stretching their hearts and minds to the limits of what the scriptures teach. One of the most important ways that we can do this is by taking seriously what we are praying when we stand at the Lord's table.

How you address God, the particular benefit of Calvary that you specifically affirm, and how you invoke the empowering and indwelling presence of the Holy Spirit are all teaching moments for the community of faith gathered about the Lord's table each week. It is important that your own understanding of the Lord's supper as an elder be informed by the breadth of scripture and the richness of Christian tradition.

A helpful resource for beginning this process of theological formation is the 1991 "Word to the Church on the Lord's Supper," the Report of the Committee on Theology that can be found in The Church for Disciples of Christ: Seeking to be Truly Church Today, edited by Paul Crow and Jim Duke. In this word from some of the best and most respected teachers of our church to our church, five biblical meanings of the Lord's supper are discussed in some detail: (1) Remembrance; (2) Communion of the Faithful; (3) Sacrifice; (4) Unity; and (5) the Feast of the Kingdom of God. Their discussion of these five themes is a theologically sound and denominationally appropriate place to begin the process of enlarging your understanding of what we are doing at the Lord's table each Sunday morning. The eleven themes for the communion prayers that follow here are an expansion of this, our resolve to speak where the Bible speaks. Each category represents a different biblical facet of the significance of the Lord's supper for us as people of faith.

REMEMBRANCE

For the Bread

Breaking the bread here this morning, Eternal God, takes us back to an upper room on the eve of a turbulent day long ago when your Son laid down his life in love for the whole world. But it's so much more than just history that we mark by this act of remembrance at this table. Here we touch the very source of our redemption and receive the present benefits of Calvary. And so may your Spirit now make the vital connection between what happened one Friday afternoon on a hill outside of Jerusalem long ago and the deepest needs of our hearts opened up to you here this morning. This we pray in the name of he who is the same yesterday, today, and forever. Amen.

Biblical Allusion—Hebrews 13:8

For the Cup

Jesus blessed and shared a cup with his disciples on the night before he died, Loving God, calling it "the cup that is poured out for you [in] the new covenant in my blood." We were not there on that night of its institution long ago, but because of that new covenant established by the shedding of Christ's blood on Calvary's cross, we have access to that upper room right now in a very real way. Not having seen him, yet we believe in him, and this morning, by your Spirit, the reality of Christ's presence becomes part of the history of this moment in the life of this community gathered here around the table, in Jesus' name. Amen.

Biblical Allusions—Luke 22:20; 1 John 1:1–3; 1 Peter 1:8

THE FORGIVENESS OF SINS

For the Bread

Holy God, you have searched and known us. Your Spirit convicts us of all unrighteousness. We know who we are and what we've done; and how we've not kept faith with you or our values in all of the moments of this week just past. If you're keeping count of the number of times and the variety of ways that we've failed you, then Lord God we're through here. But you are the One who has told us that there is always forgiveness with you, and that you will not turn away a contrite heart. And so what we offer you in this moment is the brokenness of spirit that cries out, "God, be merciful to us, sinners." And gladly and gratefully what we take from your hand is this piece of broken bread, emblematic of Christ's body that was broken for our forgiveness. Amen.

Biblical Allusions: Psalm 139:1; John 16:8; Psalm 130:3–4; Psalm 51:17; Luke 11:13

For the Cup

God of Grace, as we drink from this cup that represents to us the shed blood of our Savior Jesus Christ, startle us again with how we got here. We know that we have no right to come to this table. We know that we have no claims on this cup. And we know that we do not deserve the sacrifice that it signifies. It is only because your Word and your Spirit invite us that we come. And we approach your presence by the new and living way that has been opened up for us by Jesus Christ, our great High Priest, who cleanses us from every sin. Amen.

Biblical Allusions: Revelation 22:17; Hebrews 10:19–22

THE PRESENCE OF CHRIST

For the Bread

Hidden God, most of the time we grope in the darkness hoping to make contact with you. We follow our best hunches and guesses, deciphering the clues that you leave for us in creation and conscience. We are accustomed to seeing in the mirror dimly at best, but then there come those blessed moments of absolutely clarity. This morning we thank you for the way that we know you through the breaking of this bread. And so as we sit again at your table this morning, as the bread is taken, blessed, broken, and given, open our eyes and let us recognize you as the companion who journeys with us. And please send your Spirit afresh into our hearts in this moment of communion so that we might know that we are never alone. Amen.

Biblical Allusions—Acts 14:15–17; 17:24–28;
1 Corinthians 13:12; Luke 24:30–31; John 4:16–18

For the Cup

It's here at this table, Revealing God, that we "see thee face to face." It's here that we "touch and handle things unseen." We thank you that the cup we bless at your table here this morning is a sharing in the blood of Christ that gives us eternal life. As we drink from it deeply, quenching our great thirst for you, fill us anew with your Holy Spirit so that from our hearts may flow rivers of living water by which you will renew the earth. Amen.

Biblical Allusions—1 Corinthians 10:16; John 6:54;
John 7:37–39; Ezekiel 47

Hymn Allusion—"Here, O My Lord, I See Thee
Face to Face," Chalice Hymnal *no. 416 (v. 1)*

THANKSGIVING

For the Bread

God of Generosity and Grace, you love the world so much that you gave your only begotten Son. We come to this table this morning to break this bread and give thanks because we believe in him and have received the gift of life, both abundant and eternal. Freely receiving, now move us by your Spirit within to freely give. Loved, help us to be loving; forgiven, help us to be forgiving; reconciled, help us to be reconciling. God of grace make us people of gratitude, we pray in the name of Jesus Christ, your best gift of all. Amen.

Biblical Allusions—John 3:16; John 10:10; Matthew 10:8;
1 John 4:11, 19; Ephesians 4:32

For the Cup

Great God, because you love us so, our cup overflows and our joy is full. This morning this table of remembrance is our altar of thanksgiving and this cup of blessing is our cup of rejoicing. Send your Spirit in special measure in this hour that we might not forget any of the benefits of the cross: the forgiveness of sins, our reconciliation to you and to others; freedom from what has held us in bondage; the healing of what has been broken; hope for eternity and strength for today. For all of these things, and so much more that your love displayed in Jesus Christ reveals, we give you thanks this day in his name. Amen.

Biblical Allusions—Psalm 23:5; John 16:24; Psalm 103:1–5

OBEDIENCE

For the Bread

Commanding God, we gather here at your table to break this bread in remembrance of your Son Jesus Christ our Lord, because he told us to do so on that night long ago in the upper room. Now, as we conform in obedience here to Christ's table command, search our lives with your Spirit and show us of any area of disobedience in our lives of discipleship. Because we want to know and do all that Christ has commanded, save us from the kind of ceremonial obedience that strains at the minutiae of ritual and misses altogether the weightier matters of your word, will, and ways, we pray. Amen.

Biblical Allusions—Matthew 28:20; 23:23

For the Cup

Revealing and Directing God, your word tells us that Jesus Christ learned obedience through what he suffered, and thereby became the source of eternal salvation for all who now obey him. In the upper room Jesus told his disciples that, "This cup that is poured out for you is the new covenant in my blood." But then immediately after in the Garden of Gethsemane, Jesus prayed, "Remove this cup from me; yet, not my will but yours be done." Today as we share that cup of the new covenant in his blood, may your Spirit be our teacher. May we see in this struggle of your Son our own struggle to be your obedient people in all things, we pray. Amen.

Biblical Allusions—Hebrews 5:7–10; Luke 22:20; 22:42

MISSION

For the Bread

Giving God, you so loved the world that you gave your only begotten Son so that whoever believed in him would not perish but have eternal life. And so it was that when he was here, your Son, Jesus Christ, our Lord, picked up the cross and then laid down his life as the atoning sacrifice for our sins, and not for ours only, but also for the sins of the whole world. Today as we break this bread in remembrance of the way that Christ gave himself for us, remind us that there's a cross for us to bear as well, and a world to love and serve in Christ's name. As you sent him, so now send us inspired by his example and empowered by his Spirit. Amen.

Biblical Allusions—John 3:16; 1 John 2:2; John 20:21;
Matthew 16:24; 28:19

For the Cup

Serving God, on the night that Jesus Christ was betrayed, he took a cup, blessed it, and then shared it with his disciples. We drink this cup here today because of the example and exhortation of Jesus to do so in remembrance of him. We gather here every week to drink this cup in remembrance of him. But lest we forget, this morning remind us that before blessing the cup that night, Jesus first girded himself with a towel and knelt down to wash his disciples' feet. He did this as an example and exhortation that we should wash feet, too. Send your Spirit in this time of communion this morning that we might see the feet of those you intend for us to wash today: the poor, the sick, the abused, the neglected, the persecuted, the outcasts, the forgotten, the imprisoned. Whenever we drink this cup in remembrance of Christ, send us to our knees to wash feet in remembrance of him as well, we pray. Amen.

Biblical Allusions—John 13:1–20; Matthew 25:31–46

WITNESS

For the Bread

We believe that Jesus is the Christ, your Son, O Living God. And we know him to be both our Lord and our Savior. And so as we draw near to this table here this morning to break this bread in remembrance of him and his sacrificial death, we come bringing Christ our sins that need his forgiving as the Savior and our lives that need his directing as the Lord. As we take, bless, break, and eat this bread, may our participation be a proclamation of what we truly believe. Send your Spirit to empower this witness, for by sharing this bread we are proclaiming Christ's death until he comes again in glory. Amen.

Biblical Allusions—Matthew 16:16; Acts 1:8;
1 Corinthians 11:26

For the Cup

We drink this cup today, Saving God, as a way of acting on our faith in Jesus Christ your Son. He embraced Calvary's cross and willingly poured out his life's blood to show us the breadth, length, height, and depth of your love. And we share this cup together this morning to show our commitment to him. May this simple act of devotion be transformed by your empowering Spirit into a powerful proclamation of faith, so that as often as we drink this cup we are preaching from our pews the message of Christ's saving death until he comes again in glory. Amen.

Biblical Allusions—Ephesians 3:18; 1 Corinthians 11:26

UNITY

For the Bread

As we gather here at your table this morning, Loving God, to break bread and remember Jesus Christ and him crucified, open our eyes to see clearly our differences. We don't look alike. We don't think alike. We don't act alike. In fact, the only thing that draws us together in this community and that holds us together in relationship is your great love for us shown so clearly in Jesus Christ. And so as we share together this bread of remembrance, thanksgiving, and presence, draw us more tightly in the Spirit's tether, that bound to you by heart we might be better bound to one another by hands that serve, by arms that lift up in support, and by backs that gladly bear one another's burdens, we pray. Amen.

Biblical Allusions—1 Corinthians 2:2;
Galatians 6:2; Hebrews 12:12

For the Cup

As we drink from this cup here this morning, which represents to us the lifeblood of your Son, our Savior Jesus Christ, poured out so freely for us, Giving and Forgiving God, let it do its work of making us spiritually one. We've made our way to this table from different directions and by different paths, but this morning we all stand here side by side seeking the same thing at the same time. We are not different in what we need, and we are not different in what we hope. And so in this moment of holy communion, as we taste the sweetness of this drink, let us also experience the sweetness of your Spirit that makes us glad both to be here, and to be here together, we pray in Jesus' name. Amen.

Biblical Allusions—Ephesians 2:11–22

RENEWAL

For the Bread

Providing God, we open our hands and you fill them with good things. Your goodness to us is as abundant as it is undeserved. Each week we come to this table empty. We cannot stand before you boasting of our faithfulness; we can only confess our failures and faults. We come with hands as bare as our hearts, and we ask again for just a taste of the bounty of your love so richly supplied in Jesus Christ. Strengthen us with this bread broken and shared here this morning, and sustain us with your Spirit. Make us willing and pliable vessels constantly being filled and renewed by your redeeming grace, we pray. Amen.

Biblical Allusions—Psalm 104:28; Luke 18:9–14

For the Cup

As a deer longs for flowing water, so our souls thirst for you, O God. As from a dry and barren land where there is no water, we have come into your sanctuary to be refreshed and renewed. And here our cups are filled to overflowing with the abundance of your love. Before we call, you answer; and while we are still speaking you are already supplying all of our needs. Thank you for the goodness and mercy that dog our steps all the way, and that get especially focused for us in this cup of remembrance of Christ's death on Calvary's cross. As we are being renewed by your Spirit day by day, fill us with gratitude and praise, we pray. Amen.

Biblical Allusions—Psalm 42:1; Psalm 63; Psalm 23:5;
Isaiah 65:24; Psalm 23:6

COVENANT

For the Bread

Faithful God, you who have bound yourself to us by steadfast love, may our participation in this covenant meal here today be an outward and visible sign of the inward and invisible intentions of our hearts to be bound to you by a response of steadfast love in return. In the breaking of this bread we are made mindful of the broken body of your Son Jesus Christ on Calvary's cross, and we understand that he willingly took up that cross to show us the depth of your commitment to us. So now as we share this bread broken in remembrance of him, strengthen, by your indwelling and empowering Spirit, our resolve to take our stand with you no matter what may come. Let love always be our bond, we pray. Amen.

For the Cup

As we drink from this cup, Abiding and Abundant God, let your Holy Spirit wash over us afresh, renewing the covenant of love made between us, which binds us to you and one another. Strengthen the connections so that they will hold when the pressures come that would try to pull us apart. And as we cling to the cross as the sign of your faithfulness to us, assure us that the hold you have on us will not be broken. At this table here this morning, whisper in our ears in tones we can understand that blessed promise that nothing in all creation has the power to separate us from your love that we know in Christ Jesus our Lord. Amen.

Biblical Allusion—Romans 8:31–39

Hymnal Allusion—"The Preamble to the Design,"
Chalice Hymnal *no. 355*

HOPE

For the Bread

We've heard about a feast that's coming, O God of Abundant Provision, and this bread that we break here at your table today is its herald and guarantee. We thank you for the bread of life that has come down out of heaven and endures through eternal life, even Jesus Christ our Lord. Let us eat and not be hungry; let us behold him and not be afraid, always trusting that those who come to him in faith will certainly not be cast out, but will be raised up on the last day. Send your Spirit now as the earnest of your promise, and seal our hearts for eternity, we pray. Amen.

Biblical Allusions—Revelation 19:7–9; John 6:22–40;
2 Corinthians 2:21–22; 5:5

For the Cup

God, this morning we remember how Jesus told his disciples after sharing the cup of blessing with them in the upper room that he would not drink of it again until he did so anew with us in your Kingdom. O, how we long for that Kingdom to come and for your will to be done on earth as it is in heaven. And so this morning, even as we thank you for every glimpse that we catch of that coming day when there will be no more pain, tears, or death, we pray that this foretaste of the Kingdom we receive at this table will fire our imaginations and fuel our passions to begin to embody your future here and now. Amen.

Biblical Allusions—Matthew 26:26–29; 6:10; Revelation 21:3–5

3

Communion Prayers Based on Communion Hymns

For Disciples, our hymns are our liturgy. Now, that word liturgy probably needs some explaining. To those of us with a preference for freedom in our worship and spirituality, the word liturgy probably has some negative connotations. It suggests an unnecessary preoccupation with rituals and formulas. But such suspicions do not do justice to the true meaning of liturgy.

The word liturgy refers to the shared work of the people. It was not originally a religious word at all, but was rather a term that was used to talk about civic duty and action. When the people of a community gathered to address a common concern, what they did together was called "liturgy" (from the Greek: "What the people do"). When taken up by religion, liturgy is the word used to describe the common or shared elements of our worship. Liturgy is what we do together in our worship of God.

Some churches have worship books that provide their members with both the order and the content of their services of public worship. On Sunday mornings they follow the script of worship as it has been set out for them. We don't as Disciples. Alexander Campbell used to say that there is no book of Leviticus in the New Testament, that is, a book of rules and regulations for the life of our public worship. There were however, in his opinion, some common ingredients to Christian worship: the singing of hymns, songs, and spiritual songs, the reading of the scriptures and their exposition, the breaking of bread (communion), prayer, and the "fellowship" (the offering). For worship to be Christian, Alexander Campbell argued that these elements all needed to be present. But how they were ordered in a service of public worship was left up to the freedom of each and every congregation. This is why, to this day, there is no uniform order of worship from Disciples congregation to Disciples congregation.

But what we do have is a hymnal. Apart from the Lord's Prayer prayed in unison and some kind of responsive reading printed in the weekly bulletin, the only time we join our voices together as one in the typical Disciples worship service is when we sing. And one of the moments when we regularly sing together as Disciples is as we come to the service of the Lord's table. Because our prayers at the Lord's table often follow the congregational singing of a communion hymn, there is a spiritual logic and power in the practice of drawing on the words, phrases, images, and themes expressed in the communion hymn for our communion prayers as elders. The prayers that follow here are based on some of the standard hymns found in the *Chalice Hymnal,* which many of us sing each Sunday morning in our congregations as we come to the time of communion.

"LIFT HIGH THE CROSS"
Chalice Hymnal no. 108

For the Bread

Crucified God, we wear beautiful crosses around our necks and hang them on our walls. We have made your "triumphant sign" of suffering decorative, when what it really needs to be is defining. So make us cruciform, Lord. In our weekly remembrance of Christ's death on the cross in the breaking of this bread, let us not be content with the promise of "life eternally" alone. But push us by your Spirit to bear "on the brow the seal of Christ who died," and to show by the offerings of our hearts and hands the depth of our commitment to live for him who died for us. In lives of sacrifice and service empower our witness to Jesus Christ whose cross so powerfully proclaims your love. Amen.

For the Cup

In lifting this cup of remembrance here this morning, O God of Sacrifice, we are lifting high the cross of Christ and proclaiming your great love. We partake, with gratitude, of all the gifts that are ours in Christ crucified—new life, real unity, eternal life, and a meaningful purpose. Fill us now again with the power of your Spirit that we might be bold in our witness to Jesus Christ "till all the world adore his sacred name." Amen.

"WHEN I SURVEY THE WONDROUS CROSS"
Chalice Hymnal no. 195

For the Bread

O God of Infinite Wisdom and Unfathomable Grace, there is nothing that we could give you that would begin to repay you for the "love so amazing, so divine" that we see when we "survey the wondrous cross on which the Prince of glory died." In this bread that we break here today in remembrance of Christ's giving of himself on the cross, help us to also hear and heed the challenge to become living sacrifices in grateful response. As we offer you now our soul, our life, our all, we pray that your Spirit poured out in fresh measure will enkindle in us the fire of devotion and the passion of sacrifice after Christ's example and in Christ's name. Amen.

For the Cup

The brutality of the cross brings us up short every time, O Loving God. We are unaccustomed to and uncomfortable with gazing upon the bloodied head, hands, and feet of the Crucified One. We instinctively flinch and try to turn away from the brutality of it all. But let not our aversion to the violence of Christ's death turn us away from the "sorrow and love [that] flow mingled down." In this cup that is the emblem of that sacrifice of Christ's blood, let us taste the sorrow and be refreshed by the love that it represents. And fill us with that same Spirit of sorrow and love that our lives might be poured out to Christ in a sacrifice of eternal gratitude. Amen.

"BENEATH THE CROSS OF JESUS"
Chalice Hymnal no. 197

For the Bread

God our Rock, it is in the shadow of Christ's cross that we make our home. It is here that we find the rest and shade that we need from the glare of the searching sun at noonday. Exposed, we need to be shielded; weary, we need to be relieved. And these things we find beneath the cross of Jesus. Today as we break the bread in remembrance of and thanksgiving for what you did for us in Jesus Christ on Calvary, teach us how to abide always in you and to find our glory in the cross. Feed us by this bread and sustain us by your Spirit, we pray. Amen.

For the Cup

We bless and share this cup, Abiding God, so that our eyes can focus more clearly on "the very dying form of one who suffered" on the cross for us. But it's more than a history lesson that we need here today. And so touch our hearts in their depths by this powerful remembrance of Christ's death on Calvary's cross. By your Spirit, in this moment of communion, break our hearts with the knowledge of our unworthiness, and then startle us again with the wonder of your redeeming love so that beneath Christ's cross we would forever take our stand. Amen.

"WERE YOU THERE"
Chalice Hymnal no.198

For the Bread

We were not there when they crucified your Son, Lord God. But here at this table every week we gather to remember that Friday afternoon long ago when he was crucified. We take the bread and break it. We think about what happened to Christ on the cross and what it means for us sitting here today. But we don't often tremble. So *"tremble us"* this morning, Lord. "Tremble us," Lord, because of what Christ did, and because Christ did it for us. "Tremble us," Lord, because we dare not take any of this for granted and thereby presume upon your grace. "Tremble us," Lord, down to the center of our beings where we are touched and transformed, we beg. Amen.

For the Cup

Some were there when Jesus Christ was crucified, O God, who did not tremble. Soldiers were there, unaware that it was Your Son who was dying on their cross. A crowd of people was there, many of whom were just along for the show, who didn't have a clue that it was your salvation that was unfolding before their very eyes. Leaders were there preoccupied with their power and position. They didn't tremble, Lord. As we share this cup filled with the wine that is emblematic of the blood that was shed that day, send your Spirit so that we might tremble. We are not unlike those who did not tremble long ago. Just like them, we can miss the significance of what you did for us in Jesus Christ. Open our eyes and hearts here this morning. Cause us to tremble, and then deepen that trembling into thanksgiving, and distill that thanksgiving into transformation, we pray. Amen.

"O SACRED HEAD, NOW WOUNDED"
Chalice Hymnal no. 202

For the Bread

"What language shall [we] borrow to thank thee, dearest Friend?" When we were dead in our sin, lost in our rebellion, far from home in that distant country, you came in Jesus Christ to seek and save us. Around this table where we break the bread in remembrance and thanksgiving each week of how you came and what you did, let us see—with the eyes of our hearts—Jesus Christ publicly exhibited as crucified. And in the power of your Spirit, help us to make the personal application of Christ's "dying sorrow" to our lives so that we might be "thine forever" and never "outlive [our] love" for you. Amen.

Biblical Allusions—Ephesians 2:1; Romans 5:10;
Luke 15:13; Luke 19:10; Galatians 3:1

For the Cup

The crown of thorns on Christ's "sacred head," God of Suffering Love, reminds us of your passion. What you suffered in Jesus Christ on Calvary's cross "was all for sinners' gain." Ours "was the transgression," but yours "the deadly pain." The mystery of this transaction of mercy exceeds our capacity to understand. All we can do is fall before you in wonder and praise, thanking you for "thy favor" and asking to be kept "in thy grace." Sharing this cup today in remembrance of the "sacred head" of your Son "with grief and shame weighed down" for us, let us also be sharers of your Spirit so that our "fainting" might be changed to faith, and your passion become the source of our devotion, we pray in Jesus' name. Amen.

"IN THE CROSS OF CHRIST I GLORY"
Chalice Hymnal no. 207

For the Bread

We come to your table each week, God of Truth and Love, needing reorientation. Between Sundays we live through days "when the woes of life" threaten to overwhelm us, and where "hopes deceive" and "fears annoy." In the wreckage of decisions made, dreams dashed, confidences shaken, and trusts broken, we need to find something that is sure. Here at this table where "the light of sacred story" "glows with peace and joy," we find our unshaken and unshakeable foundation. We eat this bread in remembrance of Christ because it is in his cross that we glory. Fed at your table and filled with your Spirit, let us draw both strength and courage for the days ahead. And then draw us back again to this table where the cross of Christ stands "towering over the wrecks of time." Amen.

Biblical Allusions—Romans 8:38–39; John 14:18

For the Cup

God of all our days, the good and the bad, those filled with joy and those touched with sorrow, help us to find our true meaning not in the changing circumstances of our lives but in the cross of Christ. As we share this cup that by faith links us to Christ's sacrifice, sanctify our "bane and blessing," our "pain and pleasure." On those days when "the sun of bliss is beaming light," teach us how to glory in the cross of Christ. And on those days when "the woes of life overtake" us, teach us how to glory in the cross of Christ. What we need most is a peace at the center "that knows no measure," and a joy "that through all time abide[s]." As our hearts are drawn again to the cross this morning in the blessing of this cup, touch them with your Spirit so that they will glow "with peace and joy" in Jesus Christ, we pray. Amen.

"HERE AT THY TABLE, LORD"
Chalice Hymnal no. 384

For the Bread

If faith is the substance of things hoped for and the evidence of things not seen, Invisible God, then this table is our weekly exercise in faith. Unseen, you nevertheless speak to us here, we believe, as our host. And unheard, we believe in "pardon and peace." And so, it is our prayer of faith here this morning that you will *"sit at the feast, dear Lord,"* "break... the bread," and "feed us." Touch each "common day" "with thy pierced hands," and fill our earthly lives with your grace. By your indwelling Spirit let us "feel thee near in loving power," and hold us "till in the home of heaven we find our place," we pray in Jesus' powerful name. Amen.

Biblical Allusion—Hebrews 11:1

For the Cup

We drink from this cup filled with mercy from the hands of Jesus Christ, Present God, because we are so thirsty. We thirst for life because we live in the shadow of death. We thirst for peace because we live in a world of chaos. We thirst for pardon because we know the brokenness of our own sin. And we thirst for release because we feel the chains of bondage that hold us tight. Unable to quench any of these needs from our own reserves, by the Spirit we gratefully hear the invitation of Jesus Christ your Son, our Host, to enter this banquet hall, to come to this table, to sit at this feast and to drink from this cup "that brings life to the dead." "Fill thou the cup," Lord, we humbly pray. Amen.

"ONE BREAD, ONE BODY"
Chalice Hymnal **no. 393**

For the Bread

Just as these pieces of bread came from a single loaf, One God in Three Persons, so we who are many become one people in your love: "Gentile or Jew, servant or free, woman or man." We thank you for the "one bread, one body, one Lord of all" whose presence we experience and whose sacrifice we remember with thanksgiving at this table. Continue to push us by your inclusive love in Jesus Christ so that we will make every effort to maintain the unity of the Spirit in the bond of peace. Remind us every time that we gather at this table where we are made one by your love, that the world is looking at our unity and making decisions about the truth of the gospel by what is seen. May they see Christ. Amen.

Biblical Allusions—1 Corinthians 10:17; Romans 12:4–5;
Galatians 3:27–28; Ephesians 4:3; John 17:20–21

For the Cup

There is "one cup of blessing which we bless," O God from whom all blessings flow, and it is the cup of the new covenant made possible in Christ's blood. As we bless it here at your table this morning, bless us in Jesus Christ with every spiritual blessing: the blessing of being chosen by you; the blessing of being adopted as your children; the blessing of redemption through Christ's blood, the blessing of an inheritance of hope; and the blessing of having heard the word of truth in the gospel. Marked now with the seal of the promised Holy Spirit as the pledge of all these blessings, bring to mind the crucial truth that we have been so blessed in Jesus Christ to be a blessing. Amen.

Biblical Allusion—Ephesians 1:3–14

"WHEN YOU DO THIS, REMEMBER ME"
Chalice Hymnal no. 400

For the Bread

Sharing together this bread of remembrance from your table today, O God from whom every family in heaven and on earth takes its name, draw tight the bond of our spiritual kinship with each other through the loving sacrifice of Jesus Christ and the empowering presence of the Holy Spirit. Looking to Christ, who emptied himself and became the servant of all by his death on the cross, show us how to look to the interests of others. "Embraced together in God's arms," help us now to embrace each other in our arms as well. And rejoicing with those who rejoice, and weeping with those who weep, link our lives together as one family in your love so that we can honor Jesus Christ our Lord and Savior. Amen.

Biblical Allusions—Ephesians 3:14;
Philippians 2:1–10; Romans 12:15

For the Cup

God of New Beginnings and Second Chances, we remember our Lord Jesus Christ in the sharing of this cup from your table. May our sharing in the blood of Christ "renew our faith" so that we might hold fast to our "strong hope," "unshaken to the end." "Indebted" to your love in Jesus Christ, move us from isolation to community. Because we have been "brought home into [your] family" and been made one people through Jesus Christ, by your Spirit enable us to lift drooping hands, strengthen weak knees, straighten paths for tired feet, and carry lame brothers and sisters so that no one fails to obtain the grace of God that is ours through Jesus Christ our Lord. Amen.

Biblical Allusion—Hebrews 12:12–15

"IN REMEMBRANCE OF ME"
Chalice Hymnal no. 403

For the Bread

Commanding God, we come to this table each week, we break the bread, and we give you thanks as we remember the sacrifice of Jesus Christ your Son. We cherish this table and its precious supper because it is here that we know that you can always be found. But this morning send your Holy Spirit to bring to our remembrance the other things that you told us to do and the promises of other places where you assured us that you could be found. In remembrance of Jesus Christ and in anticipation of meeting him there, send us to heal the sick, to feed the poor, and to open the door to let the neighbor in. By being with you here, help us to see you there, we pray. Amen.

Biblical Allusion—Matthew 25:31–46

For the Cup

O God, who has given us the knowledge of your glory in the face of Jesus Christ, keep us now from looking for you in all the wrong places. Draw us here to your table each week, where we can drink the wine in remembrance of Christ and his precious blood shed for us. And in this act of faith, ground our search for the truth. Cue your Spirit to bear witness with our spirits so that we can cry out, "Abba! Father!" Prompt us to love you and one another as the surest sign that we know you and are committed to your ways. In remembrance of Christ, keep us from looking above for you, but in our own hearts to actually find you, we pray. Amen.

Biblical Allusions—2 Corinthians 4:6; Romans 8:15

"COME, SHARE THE LORD"
Chalice Hymnal no. 408

For the Bread

Present God, we "take the bread" this morning with the great expectation that we will "share the Lord." Gathering in Jesus' name, we want him to "join us here" as "our gracious host." With all our hearts we believe that "though unseen he meets us here in the breaking of the bread." Once again send your Spirit so that "His love" will be "burning in our hearts like living flame." Empower us to be forgiving so that we might live with the continuing experience of his presence in the unity of this community which prays in the name of "the one we love the most," Jesus Christ our Lord. Amen.

Biblical Allusions—1 Corinthians 10:16–17; 12:12–13

For the Cup

Future God, when we gather at this table each Sunday morning we are not only filled with gratitude, we are filled with longing. We long for another gathering "where angels sing." We long to see "the glory of our Lord and coming King." And we long for that heavenly "feast for which we wait" and to which this cup points. You gave us this cup to drink so that we could "share the Lord" until that day when he comes again in glory, and you fill us with the Spirit so that we might have the assurance that the promises you have made are the promises that you will keep. We are glad to have these guarantees of that future. But still we long. We long for you. We long to see you and to know you just as we have been fully known by you. As we drink the cup of remembrance here this morning, bring us closer to the day when we shall eat at the heavenly banquet forever. Amen.

Biblical Allusions—2 Corinthians 5:5; 1:20;
1 Corinthians 13:12; Psalm 23:6; Revelation 19:9

"WE PLACE UPON YOUR TABLE, LORD"
Chalice Hymnal no. 417

For the Bread

Mysterious God, ordinary objects hold your grace and common experiences express your glory. You, the God beyond all our imaginings, show yourself in the most mundane of ways. Here is a table, and there is a loaf of bread. But here the table becomes an altar; here the bread becomes a sign of your presence. As we take it, break it, bless it, and share it, Jesus Christ becomes known by us anew. Send your Spirit that this table may be our meeting place this morning, and this bread the emblem of Christ's body broken for us. Come to us through these tokens of our daily work and human life, and receive our thanks for making yourself known to us in the breaking of the bread. Amen.

For the Cup

It took work to make the wine that we drink here this morning, Companion God. Somebody had to harvest the grapes. Somebody had to press them into juice. Somebody had to package and deliver the product to us. And somebody here had to prepare the communion trays. What we will consume so quickly took somebody else hours, days, weeks, and months to prepare. We so rarely calculate that cost, O Lord. The wine we drink here this morning is the sign of your Son's precious blood spilled for us. That was work too: thirty-three years of sacrifice and service—beginning in manger, ending on a cross, and being transformed in a garden tomb. Let us not take any of "your grand design" for granted. At this table where this morning we place "the food of life, the bread and wine," make us grateful for all the work that goes into it, both ours and yours. Amen.

"I COME WITH JOY"
Chalice Hymnal no. 420

For the Bread

Help us to come and go with joy from your table today, Gracious God. Instead of the condemnation that our sins so justly deserve, in the breaking of the bread that points to the atoning sacrifice of Jesus Christ on the cross fill our hearts with the joy of knowing that we are "forgiven, loved and free." Instead of the somber service of penance that the Lord's supper has so often become in our practice, today let it be a sheer celebration of the love "laid down" for us in the life and death of Jesus Christ our Savior. And as joy is one of the surest signs of your presence, so fill us with your Spirit here this morning that the joy of our salvation in Jesus Christ is something that we both experience in ourselves and express to those around us in loving ways, we pray. Amen.

For the Cup

It is here at this table each week that we know that we are loved, Generous God. It is here that we gather with Christians "far and near" to hear again the story of the gospel. And when we take the cup and bless it to recall "the life of Jesus... in love laid down" for us, we become one with all that love includes. And in that love that makes us one, "each proud division ends" as strangers become friends. As we come to this table we become a "new community of love" through everything that you have done for us in Christ. And now, by the power of your Spirit in our hearts, send us from this table back into the world that we might offer to all this "love that makes us one," we pray in Jesus' name. Amen.

"I'M GONNA EAT AT THE WELCOME TABLE"
Chalice Hymnal no. 424

For the Bread

This morning, Welcoming God, we rejoice in having a place in your family and at this table. You have welcomed us in Jesus Christ. As we break this bread in remembrance of him here this morning, we join hands with each other as sisters and brothers as we share company with him. As he serves us by his living, dying, and living again, so let us serve each other by the power of his Spirit within us. And as we eat at this welcome table here this morning, make us painfully aware of those who are not here, who are not welcomed by the standards of the world but who have already been welcomed by your grace, if not by your people. Welcomed, inspire us to be welcoming, we pray. Amen.

Biblical Allusions—Romans 15:7–9; 14:7–9

For the Cup

Once we were not a people, but now we are your people, O God. Once we knew no mercy, but now we have received your mercy in Jesus Christ. Once we were without his companionship, aliens from his community, and strangers to his promises, without hope and without you. But now, in Jesus Christ, we who once were far off have been brought near by his blood. And we take, bless, and share this cup here this morning in remembrance of that blood and its power to break down the dividing walls and to give us access in the one Spirit to you. No longer strangers, but members of your family by grace, open our eyes and hearts to any who wander this morning far from the experience of your love in Jesus Christ. Familiar with the pain of that isolation, keep us sensitive to the pain of that isolation. And as we have been welcomed here to this table by the grace seen in the shedding of Christ's blood, make us just as welcoming as we have been welcomed by him in whose name we pray, Jesus Christ. Amen.

Biblical Allusions—1 Peter 2:9;
Ephesians 2:11–21; Romans 15:7

4

Communion Prayers
for the Church Year

There is a familiar rhythm to the year. The cold of winter
gives way to the promise of spring. The heat of summer
withers the fresh growth of spring and parches the once lush
ground. Fall brings a change of temperature and lengthening
of shadows. And then the cold, wet winds of winter blow
again. We have changes of wardrobe and a cycle of celebrations to mark each passing season, and the church does too.

The Church Year is a way of teaching the Christian faith.
It begins with Advent (from the Latin for "coming"), the four
weeks before Christmas. This is a season of promise and hope,
penitence and preparation, waiting and watching. Its traditional color is purple. With a burst of song and light, Advent
gives way to Christmastide at midnight on Christmas Eve.
The color is white. The Savior has come; joy to the world!
Twelve days later it's Epiphany (from the Greek for "manifes-
tation"). The color of this season is green. On successive
Sundays in this accordion season (it stretches from January
6 to Ash Wednesday, no matter how long that may be) the
true identity of that baby born in Bethlehem's manger begins
to get disclosed in stories that provide us with glimpses into
Christ's divine nature. The forty days of Lent (from the Old
English for "spring") are a season of preparation for Easter.

Just as in Advent, the other penitential season of the church year, the color for Lent is purple; and the mood is somber and reflective. Palm Sunday marks the beginning of Passion Week, the most intensive week of worship in the Church Year. The "Triduum" (from the Latin for "three days") ushers us into the heart of the mystery of the gospel: the death, burial, and resurrection of Jesus Christ. Maundy Thursday (Maundy from the Latin for "mandate" or "command") is about what happened in the upper room. Good Friday is about what happened on the cross. And Holy Saturday is about the silence of the garden tomb. The season of Easter breaks like the dawn on the Sunday morning after Good Friday. The color is white, and the message is triumph. Easter is not just a single day of the Church Year but a season lasting a full forty days until Ascension Thursday. And then, ten days later, it's Pentecost, the coming of the promised Holy Spirit and the birthday of the church. The color is red, and the mood is passionate. And then finally comes that long stretch of the Church Year until Advent rolls around again in late November or early December. This "ordinary" season is variously known as "Kingdomtide," "Trinity," or simply "The Season after Pentecost." The color is green, and the theme is growth. This is when the church has traditionally emphasized the teachings of Jesus Christ.

The communion prayers that you will find in this section follow the rhythm and try to honor the spirit of the traditional church year.

COMMUNION PRAYERS FOR ADVENT
The First Sunday of Advent: *Hope*

For the Bread

Promise-making and promise-keeping God, we come to this table this morning because of the promise that you will meet us here in the breaking of the bread. Sometimes walking by faith and not by sight takes everything we've got. We endure long stretches of life with precious few signs of your companionship and care. And so we thank you this morning for this table where we can remember your promises and for this bread broken—by which we can taste again your faithfulness in the life and death of Jesus Christ, your Son, our Savior. Nourish our hope this morning by the sign of bread and the stirring of your Spirit, we pray expectantly in his name. Amen.

Biblical Allusions—Luke 24:30–31; 2 Corinthians 5:7

For the Cup

Faithful God, this cup is proof that you keep your word. All of your promises find their fulfillment in Jesus Christ our Lord, crucified, risen, and exalted evermore. And so this morning we lift this cup and drink it as an expression of our gratitude. Tasting your trustworthiness again this morning, help us strengthen our own resolve to be people of promise committed to knowing and doing your will here on earth just as it is in heaven. You have not given us a Spirit of fear or timidity, and so empower us to be a community of grace and truth, just like our Lord, in whose name we pray. Amen.

Biblical Allusions—2 Corinthians 1:20;
Matthew 6:10; 2 Timothy 1:7

The Second Sunday of Advent: *Peace*

For the Bread

Still us for just a moment at this table here this morning, O Lord. The noise of battle and the clash of conflict sound about us, and within us. Peace is precious but so elusive. And so as we break this bread this morning, remind us that one of the gifts that Christ's death brings to us is the offer of peace. On Calvary's cross he broke down the barrier of the dividing wall and preached peace to those who were far off and to those who were near. Now having peace with you through that sacrifice, by your indwelling Spirit, let us know the peace within that is the sure fruit of your divine presence, and help us to become peacemakers, which is now part of our mission as your daughters and sons, we pray in the name of him who is our peace, Jesus Christ. Amen.

Biblical Allusions—Psalm 46:10; Ephesians 2:13–16;
Galatians 5:22; Matthew 5:9

For the Cup

God of Shalom, in this season when we anticipate the angelic song of peace and goodwill, we come to this table in remembrance of him whose shed blood is the power of that reconciliation. Christ's death for us while we were still trapped in the rebellion of our sin proves just how much you love us. You sought us while we were strangers wandering far from your fold. Jesus rescued us from danger, interposing his precious blood. And so this morning as we share this cup together, our prayer is one of thanksgiving and commitment. Even as we joyfully renew our own reconciliation with you here this morning at this table, we are mindful of that door through which we will soon pass into the world where you expect us to exercise the ministry of reconciliation. Renew us by sign and Spirit here so that we will be sensitive and faithful there, we pray in Jesus' name. Amen.

Biblical Allusions—Luke 2:14; Romans 5:6–8;
2 Corinthians 5:18–20

Hymn Allusion—"Come, Thou Fount of Every Blessing"
—Chalice Hymnal no. 16 (v. 2)

The Third Sunday of Advent: *Love*

For the Bread

As we take, bless, break, and share this bread here at your table this morning, O God, remind us again just how costly your love really is, and always will be. Talk is cheap. And so Christ emptied himself of glory, became our servant, took up the cross, and became obedient in death. He didn't just talk about love; Christ embodied love in his life and in his death. As we touch and taste this broken bread symbolic of Christ's broken body on Calvary's cross, by your Spirit stiffen our own resolve to be people who love not just with our words, but in our actions. By remembering Christ's cross of love here at this table this morning, inspire us to take up ours, and follow in his steps, we pray. Amen.

Biblical Allusions —Philippians 2:5–8; 1 John 3:18;
Matthew 16:24; 1 Peter 2:21

For the Cup

Loving God, the poet wrote, "Love came down at Christmas, love all lovely, love divine; Love was born at Christmas; star and angels gave the sign." On this third Sunday of Advent as we take and drink this cup, startle us again with this truth from the very heart of the gospel. It was because you loved the world so much that Christ came and died for us. By your Spirit, emblazon on this cup of forgiveness, and every gospel ordinance, the message of your love; and kindle it anew in every receptive heart gathered around this table here this morning. Loved, let us love, we pray in the name of the love that was born at Christmas and then grew up to offer itself fully and freely on Calvary's cross, even Jesus Christ our Savior. Amen.

Biblical Allusions—John 3:16; 1 John 4:19

Poem Allusion—"Love Came Down at Christmas"
by Christina Rossetti

The Fourth Sunday of Advent: *Joy*

For the Bread

O God, who delights in surprising us with grace and delighting us with abundance, lift our hearts again this morning at the announcement of the good news of a great joy that, born for us and for all in the city of David, is a Savior who is Christ the Lord. In this season of crèche and carol, keep our sights always on Calvary and its cross. Broken and shared, may this bread nourish and sustain us to eternal life through the work of your Spirit in our hearts. Feed us until we want no more, and then inspire us to gather up what remains so that we can offer it to a world that is desperately hungry, too. More than the bread that perishes, give us the bread of life to eat and to share, we pray in the name of Jesus, the bread come down from heaven that gives life to the world. Amen.

Biblical Allusions—Luke 2:8–15; John 6

Hymn Allusion—"Fill My Cup, Lord"
—Chalice Hymnal no. 351 (chorus)

For the Cup

This cup of gladness that we bless here today, O Generous God, is a sign of the joy that is ours as your children. We know that we are at this table only by your invitation and that we can partake of its bounty only by your gracious provision. This cup of the new covenant made possible by the blood of Jesus Christ shed for all turns our tears to laughter and our despair to joy. As this cup is filled this morning to the brim with the emblem of your love, so fill our hearts to overflowing this week with your indwelling Spirit so that love spills out and sloshes over onto all we meet, and who in Jesus Christ are loved just as much as we know ourselves to be, we pray. Amen.

Biblical Allusions—Psalm 126:5–6;
1 Corinthians 11:25; 1 John 2:2

COMMUNION PRAYERS FOR CHRISTMAS
Christmas Eve

For the Bread

O God, this is the night of angels and shepherds for which we have been waiting. How we have longed to see the light of that guiding star and to hear that familiar chorus of, "Peace on the earth, good will to all, from heaven's all gracious King." Our journey has brought us here tonight, to this table. Just as it took faith for those first visitors to find the Savior in Bethlehem's manger, so help us tonight to have the faith to be able to find the Savior in the breaking of this bread. Soften our hearts, O Holy Spirit, and clear our eyes, so that we might see this great salvation of which the prophets from long ago spoke, and into which the angels longed to look, we pray in the name of that newborn babe. Amen.

Biblical Allusions: Matthew 2:1–2; Luke 2:8–14; 1 Peter 1:10–12

> *Hymn Allusion—"It Came upon a Midnight Clear"*
> — Chalice Hymnal *no. 153 (v. 1)*

For the Cup

"To show God's love aright, [Mary] bore to us a Savior when half spent was the night." And this is the hour, O God, when we attend to the details of that birth as spiritual midwives. Just as Christ was born so long ago in Bethlehem's manger, so may he be born again tonight in each one of our hearts. This cup that we bless now is an emblem of the blood that he shared with us as our human companion on the path of life of this world, and shed for us as our Divine Savior in order to open the gate to eternal life. By your Holy Spirit, may that blood never lose its power to bind you to us, us to you, and us to one another, we pray in the name of him whose birth we celebrate tonight. Amen.

Biblical Allusion: Hebrews 2:14–15

> *Hymn Allusions—"Lo, How a Rose E'er Blooming "*
> — Chalice Hymnal *no. 160 (v. 2);*
> *"The Blood Will Never Lose Its Power"*
> — Chalice Hymnal *no. 206*

Christmas Day

For the Bread

On this special day of gift giving and gift receiving, we remember that before it all, and behind it all, is the great fact that you are a God who gives us every good and perfect gift. We know that in you we live, and move, and have our being, both physically and spiritually. Every morning we open our hands and receive with thanksgiving the daily bread that sustains our bodies. And on this Christmas morning we open our hearts and receive again with thanksgiving the bread broken in remembrance of Christ's sacrificial gift on Calvary's cross, the bread of life that sustains our souls. So nourish us with your Word and Spirit that our lives might be gifts of faithful witness and service that would prove pleasing to you always, we pray in the name of Jesus Christ, your very best gift. Amen.

Biblical Allusions—James 1:17; Acts 17:28; Matthew 6:11

For the Cup

O God, of all the gifts that will be shared among us today, none compares with the gift of your Son's lifeblood poured out for us all. Let us not become so bedazzled by the shiny trinkets or distracted with our new little luxuries of this day that we overlook the gift that this table memorializes. As we take this cup, by your Spirit help us to see how Bethlehem's baby became Calvary's sacrifice. As we drink this cup, by your Spirit help us to hear you whisper somewhere deep inside us the reassuring message of your great love for us. And as we share this cup, by your Spirit keep us so stirred up that we never rest until all have tasted and seen your love for them as well. These things we pray in Christ's name. Amen.

The Sunday after Christmas

For the Bread

You are a God who is always bigger than we think, so let these days of Christmastide enlarge our appreciation of the gift that is Jesus Christ. As there is more to Christmas than December 25, and so much more to Jesus Christ than just the stories of his nativity, so let this table here this morning provide us with the vantage point of faith to be able to see beyond the manger's scarcity, the angels' excitement, and the shepherds' visitation. Let us see why this little baby was named "Jesus" and how he came to save his people from their sins. In the bread we break here today help us to see Jesus Christ and him crucified. By your Spirit, create room in our hearts where this little baby can stretch and grow, becoming the Savior he was sent to be, and who we so desperately need, we pray. Amen.

Biblical Allusions—Matthew 1:21;
Luke 2:13–16; 1 Corinthians 2:2

For the Cup

After the frenzy of our Christmas celebrations, O God, we are grateful for this Sunday morning of quiet reflection. With all of the shopping, wrapping, giving, getting, and feasting now behind us, we are finally in that place where we can take stock of what this season really means. This cup that we now bless represents to us the blood of your Son shed for our salvation. It is staggering to think that you loved us this much. And so as we share it together here this morning, may your Spirit go to work on our hearts to "clear the chaos and the clutter" so that we might find some space to ponder the real significance of these days. Let this table and this hour be for us the still point in a season that has been way too busy; and because we have been here to share it in this community of your people, help us all to live different lives in the days ahead—lives centered on your will and ways, and always nourished by your love in Jesus Christ. Amen.

Hymn Allusion—"Come and Find the Quiet Center"
— Chalice Hymnal no. 575 (v. 1)

COMMUNION PRAYERS FOR EPIPHANY
The First Sunday of Epiphany

For the Bread

Guiding God, wise men sought the newborn king by following the light of a star, and when they found him they knelt down and offered their gifts of gold, frankincense, and myrrh. We, too, have come, drawn by the radiance he displays. And here at this table of his presence this morning we bow down, offering the gift of our allegiance to him who is our King, the gift of our obedience to him who is our Prophet, and the gift of our thanksgiving to him who is our Priest. By eating this bread we are proclaiming our faith that Jesus is the Christ, your Son, our Lord and Savior, and we welcome anew his indwelling Spirit who prompts this confession from our hearts. Help us to know him, and make him known. Amen.

Biblical Allusions—Matthew 2:11; 1 Corinthians 12:3

For the Cup

There is anguish in the story, God of Compassion and Care. The Magi escape by another route; Herod rages; and babies die. It's hard to think of such bloodshed when so recently our songs have been of nothing but peace and joy. But here we are listening to Rachel weeping for her children and watching the holy family fleeing for their lives. So draw us to your table here this morning with our eyes open wide. Sharing this cup that is the sign of Christ's blood shed on Calvary, make us mindful of all the places where innocents still suffer and violence reigns, and assure us of the coming Kingdom when all these wrongs will be set right and we will finally know the gift of shalom in all its fullness. Send your Spirit to stir the seeds of that hope in our hearts today, we pray in Jesus' name. Amen.

Biblical Allusions—Matthew 2:12–18;
Revelation 21:1–8; John 14:27

The Second Sunday of Epiphany

For the Bread

In the waters of the Jordan, Claiming God, you named Jesus as your own beloved Son, and this morning we have gathered about this table to hear you say the same thing about us. There are lots of names given to us that are designed to diminish your value and discount our place. In fact, we hear them so often that we are inclined to believe them. And so, counter those voices and contradict those labels by a clear and resounding word from you here this morning. As we take, break, bless, and share this bread that is to us the sign of Christ's body broken for us, let us hear you whisper in the ears of our hearts that we are your daughters and sons who are beloved by you, and with the eyes of our hearts let us catch a glimpse of the Spirit descending and alighting on us, forever marking us as your own, we pray. Amen.

Biblical Allusion—Matthew 3:16–17

For the Cup

"Here is the Lamb of God who takes away the sins of the world!" John cried out on the day that Jesus approached him at the Jordan River, O God. And that has been our plea ever since. At this table each week we take hold of the cup of remembrance and ponder again the wonder of Christ's blood shed for us that we might be set free from our sins. And we are amazed that he would do this for us when we were still so far from you and your ways, and had such little intention of turning around and making our way back to you. But here we are at your table today beholding the Lamb of God who takes away the sins of the world and being renewed daily by the Spirit who draws us in your love, and all we can say is thank you, thank you, thank you in Jesus' name. Amen.

Biblical Allusions—John 1:29; Romans 5:6–8

The Third Sunday of Epiphany

For the Bread

Revealing God, your Son worked his first miracle at a wedding feast—a sign and a wonder in an ordinary moment, disclosing his extraordinary identity. Forgive us for not picking up on this sanctification of the routine, and for our unbridled fascination with the unusual. While we're constantly on the alert for that remarkable and supernatural visitation, you are faithfully present in the everyday moments and the normal courses of or lives. Today at this common table we take ordinary bread, and as we bless it, break it, and share it, we discern by your Word and Spirit that it is in fact a sharing in the body of Christ. Witnesses to this weekly mystery and participants in this routine grace, we ask you to open our eyes to see you and our hearts to recognize you in all of our familiar places this week, we pray in the name of Jesus Christ. Amen.

Biblical Allusions—John 2:1–11; 1 Corinthians 10:16

For the Cup

God of Abundance and the Fullness of Joy, in Cana of Galilee Jesus turned water into wine and the hearts of all the guests were made glad. Today, at this table, in this cup, wine will become the emblem of Christ's blood shed for us as the sign of your great love, and our hearts will be made glad as well. Why you love us like this, we cannot say. But we know it by the witness of the gospel, the stirrings of your Spirit, and the transformation we are even now experiencing by your grace. It took a miracle for that water to become wine, but the greater miracle still is the way that you are changing us by the sacrifice of love this cup commemorates here this morning. Let joy be made complete, both yours and ours in this time of communion with Jesus Christ in whose name we pray. Amen.

Biblical Allusions—John 2:1–11; John 15:11

The Fourth Sunday of Epiphany

For the Bread

God of Grace and God of Glory, at the top of a mountain in Galilee you identified Jesus Christ as your Son and told us to listen to him. We are here today at your table because we believe that Jesus Christ is indeed your Son, and we have accepted him as our Lord and Savior. We break this bread as a token of his body broken for us, and as we eat it we are renewing our commitment to him and his ways. Radiance fell on that mountaintop of transfiguration in Galilee that was convincing proof to those who were present that what was unfolding before them was from you, and here today we experience a radiance in our hearts by the Holy Spirit that you have bestowed upon us that is just as convincing. Let as bask in that glory in this moment of grace, and then send us down from this mountaintop experience back into the valley of life changed by our encounter with you, in Jesus Christ our Lord. Amen.

Biblical Allusions—Matthew 17:1–12; Luke 24:32

For the Cup

So much of our lives and faith are shrouded in clouds, Hidden God. We can't see you clearly, and we can't make our way very confidently. We stumble in the confusing mist. Our progress is slow and uncertain. But these moments appear when the fog lifts and we can see what you are trying to reveal. And in those moments we get our bearings, and we set our courses to you. For some of your disciples that happened long ago on a mountaintop in Galilee, but for us it happens here at this table where the story of your Son's sacrifice for us gets told, and we drink from this cup in remembrance of his blood that was shed. We know that this time of clarity won't last long, but we are grateful for every second we have of it. And this week as we step back into the cloudy mist of confusion and uncertainty, bring to our remembrance this time of encounter with you, and let us walk in faith confidently, we pray. Amen.

Biblical Allusions—Matthew 17:1–12; Acts 17:27; John 14:26

The Fifth Sunday of Epiphany

For the Bread

Hidden God, we seek your face, and we catch glimpses of it in Jesus Christ. He teaches as one having authority. He gives sight to the blind. The wind and the waves obey him. He forgives sin. He lays down his life of his own accord, and then he has the power to take it back up again. As we gather at this table here this morning to break this bread in remembrance of him, open the eyes of our hearts by your indwelling Spirit so that we might catch fresh glimpses of you in the presence, power, and promises of Jesus Christ who is our only Lord and Savior. Amen.

Biblical Allusions—Matthew 7:28–29; 9:2–8;
Mark 4:41; John 10:18; Ephesians 1:18

For the Cup

Revealing God, take the dimness of our eyes and the dullness of our hearts away. Let us not neglect so great a salvation. May the sweetness of this taste from the cup of your salvation, full and free, restore our souls. As we drink now in remembrance of him who died for us, let us experience the fullness of your Spirit that empowers us to witness and serve. With the joy of our salvation renewed by our presence here at your table this morning, Lord, send us out as witnesses to your glory and servants of your purposes in Jesus Christ, we pray. Amen.

Biblical Allusions—Hebrews 2:3; Psalm 23:3;
Ephesians 5:18; Acts 1:8; Psalm 51:12

The Sixth Sunday of Epiphany

For the Bread

Present God, we do not always see you as clearly as we would like, and so this morning we thank you for this table where things get better focused for us. Here in the breaking of the bread Jesus Christ gets publicly exhibited as crucified. Our hearts shudder at the costliness of the sacrifice and stand amazed at the love displayed. Enlighten us in this time of communion, allow us to taste the heavenly gift, and make us sharers in the Holy Spirit, we pray. Amen.

Biblical Allusions—Galatians 3:1; Hebrews 6:4–6

For the Cup

Revealing God, in the sharing of this cup, make us eyewitnesses of your majestic glory. As we drink from this cup here this morning in remembrance of him who died for us, may the day dawn and the morning star rise in our hearts. Make us more attentive to this lamp that shines in a dark place. As the Holy Spirit moves us, kindle in us the love, joy, and peace that are the signs of your abiding presence in our hearts. Amen.

Biblical Allusions—2 Peter 1:16–21; Galatians 5:22

The Seventh Sunday of Epiphany

For the Bread

Creator God, who in the beginning divided the light from the darkness and who in Jesus Christ came as a great light dawning on those who sat in the shadow of death, this morning we thank you for being our light and our salvation. As we break this bread in remembrance of Christ's body given for us, ignite again the candles of our spirits that we might be the lamps, not hidden under the bushel basket, but placed on the table so that they might give light to all who are in the house. So fill us with your Spirit here this morning by our participation in this feast that your light will shine forth from us and that people who see us will give you the glory. Amen.

Biblical Allusions—Genesis 1:18; Matthew 4:15–16; Psalm 27:1; Proverbs 20:27; Matthew 5:14–16

For the Cup

God of Glory, whose radiance shone on the face of Moses in his encounters with you, shine in our hearts because of our encounter with you here this morning at your table. As we drink from this cup, send your Spirit so that our knowledge of your glory in the face of Jesus Christ might deepen. As John said, "The light shines in the darkness," so send your light now to shine into the darkness of our world, and do not allow the darkness to ever overwhelm us, we pray in Jesus' name. Amen.

Biblical Allusions—2 Corinthians 3:7–10; 4:6; John 1:5

COMMUNION PRAYERS FOR LENT
Ash Wednesday

For the Bread

Guiding God, in the wilderness you fed your people with manna each morning so that they would not starve. As we stand here at the edge of the wilderness of our souls for this journey of forty days, reassure us that we will be fed and sustained by you as well. Give us each day in the wilderness of this Lent our daily bread. As the Spirit drove Jesus into the wilderness after your declaration that he was your beloved Son, assure us in the breaking of the bread at this table that we are your daughters and sons, too, and then lead us by your Spirit into the place of testing and growth, we pray. Amen.

Biblical Allusions—Exodus 16:13–16; Psalm 23:5; Matthew 6:11; 3:17; 4:1

For the Cup

Providing God, in the wilderness you gave your people drink so that they would not die of thirst. As we stand here at the edge of the wilderness of our souls for this journey of forty days, reassure us that we will have something to drink when we get thirsty as well. Give us our spiritual drink from the rock that is Christ. Only because of your invitation for the thirsty to come and drink the water of life as a gift can we take the cup from your table in faith this morning. Living by the Spirit, let us also be guided by the Spirit on this journey of faith and growth through the wilderness that stretches out between us and Easter, we pray. Amen.

Biblical Allusions—Exodus 17:1–7; 1 Corinthians 10:4; Revelation 22:17; Galatians 5:25

The First Sunday of Lent

For the Bread

As we draw near to your table here this morning, Holy God, to break the bread in remembrance of how Christ's body was given for us, save us from unworthy participation. In this season of self-examination, help us to be honest with ourselves about any of those areas in our lives where we are currently contradicting your image in us by creation or your intention for us in redemption. Convict our hearts of any sin by your Holy Spirit in us this day, but keep us from condemnation by your gracious provisions for us in Jesus Christ, our Savior, we pray. Amen.

Biblical Allusions—1 Corinthians 11:27–32;
Genesis 1:17; John 16:8; Romans 8:1

For the Cup

Merciful God, it would be enough for us to get the crumbs that fall from this table. You've searched us and known us better than we've searched and known ourselves. And if we know that our sin is enough to keep us from you, then you must surely know it so much better than we do. And yet you sought us when we were far away, and you invited us in when we had no such expectation. As we share this cup here today emblematic of Christ's blood shed for sinners, reassure us again by your Spirit that we indeed belong here at your table, and to you, not because of our goodness but only because of your grace made know in Jesus Christ. Amen.

Biblical Allusions—Matthew 15:21–18;
Psalm 139:1; Luke 14:15–23

The Second Sunday of Lent

For the Bread

O God who made us and who loves us still, we know that things abide in us that do not reflect your good design. We have wrapped ourselves about with the filthy rags of our selfishness, rebellion, anger, impurity, and greed. And we see just how distorted things have become for us when we look full on the face of Jesus Christ, the new Adam. Forgive us God, and restore us. Here at your table, in the breaking of the bread this morning in remembrance of Jesus Christ given for us, fuel the continuing work of conforming us to His image by your indwelling Spirit. Help us to strip off the old humanity and empower us to put on the new self that is being renewed every day in Jesus Christ, our Lord. Amen.

Biblical Allusions—Colossians 3; Isaiah 64:6; Romans 5:14; 1 Corinthians 15:45–49; 2 Corinthians 4:16

For the Cup

You have washed us, Forgiving God, and made us clean. According to your abundant mercy, you have removed our transgressions far from us. And this cup we share here today, emblematic of Christ's blood shed for the remission of our sins, returns us each week to that place where we can confess, and know that you will be faithful and just in forgiveness. By drinking this cup, we are inviting your Spirit of holiness into our hearts anew; and we are seeking the strength we need to supply our faith with everything necessary for growth, that your call might be confirmed in us, we pray in the name of Christ who has already given us everything needful for life and godliness. Amen.

Biblical Allusions—Psalm 51:2; Hebrews 9:14; 1 John 1:7; 2 Peter 1:3–11

The Third Sunday of Lent

For the Bread

Strengthening God, we are in the place of testing and at the hour of the sifting of our souls. We have been driven into this wilderness by your Spirit, and we are being sustained only by your promises: that nothing can separate us from your love; that greater is he who is in us than he who is in the world; and that you will lose none of those who have been given into your hand. Feed us with the bread of life from your table here this morning that sustains us for the journey that remains, and go before us to show us the way home, we pray. Amen.

Biblical Allusions—1 Corinthians 10:13; Luke 22:31;
Mathew 4:1; Romans 8:38–39; 1 John 4:4; John 6:39

For the Cup

In the wilderness Jesus contended with the adversary and won, O God of power and might. We contend, too, with the struggles of flesh and blood, as well as with the unseen principalities and powers that surround us. In our own strength we stumble and fall. It is no contest. But in you, we are more than conquerors. This cup we bless here today speaks to us of the way that you did not withhold your own Son, but gave him up for us all. We take our stand in your love seen in Jesus Christ, and we know that it is not by our own might and power, but by your Spirit that we shall share your victory. Amen.

Biblical Allusions—Mark 1:12–13; Ephesians 6:10–12; Romans
8:31–39; Zechariah 4:6

The Fourth Sunday of Lent

For the Bread

On some days it seems like you are so close to us, Accompanying God, that we could stretch out our hands and touch you. But these long stretches on the journey of faith appear when we can't seem to see your face or feel your guiding and upholding hand. Wherever we happen to be this morning, in the light and joy of that felt presence, or in the long shadows of your seeming absence and silence, bring us to this table to break this bread in remembrance of Jesus Christ, who in his hours on the cross felt so abandoned that he had to cry out "My God, My God, why have you forsaken me?" yet also sensed that you were close enough for him to pray with his dying breath, "Father, into your hands I commend my spirit." Be present with us and in us by your Spirit, regardless of where we are or how we feel, we pray in Jesus' name. Amen.

Biblical Allusions—Matthew 27:46; Luke 23:46

For the Cup

"Do this in remembrance of me," your Son instructed us, O God. And sometimes remembrance is all we've got. We want your presence in our lives and in our world with power and glory. But lots of times in the silence and struggle of our faith without sight, all we have to rely upon is the memory of your faithfulness in the past and what that says about your faithfulness to come. This morning this cup is our anchor that holds within the storm. It brings to heart and mind that day long ago when Christ bore his cross to the top of dark Calvary for us. We trust its power even when we don't feel it, and we know you are there even if we can't see you at the moment. As we drink today in remembrance of him, let us feel the wind of your Spirit sweep across the barrenness of our souls, we pray in the name of him who sends the Spirit so that we will never feel abandoned or alone: Jesus Christ. Amen.

Biblical Allusions—Hebrews 6:19; Luke 22:19; John 3:8;
John 14:18; 14:27–28; 17:26

The Fifth Sunday of Lent

For the Bread

God of Patterns and of Promises, the rain of forty days and nights flooded the world and floated Noah's Ark; for forty days and nights Moses entered into the midst of the cloud to be with you on the mountaintop; for forty years our spiritual mothers and fathers wandered in the wilderness; and for forty days and nights Jesus fasted in the wilderness after his baptism. We are now drawing near to the close of the forty days of our Lent. We, too, have been tested and tried. And we, too, have been blessed and sustained by your companionship. This table has been our place of refuge, and this bread the sign of your presence with us. We break and share it today in thanksgiving for your guidance and protection in Jesus Christ. And we pray to be sustained by your Spirit until that day when our faith has become sight and we know you fully even as we are already fully known by you. Amen.

Biblical Allusions—Genesis 7:12; Exodus 24:18;
Numbers 14:33; Matthew 4:2;
2 Corinthians 5:7; 1 Corinthians 13:12

For the Cup

It's grace upon grace that we have received from Christ's fullness, O God of abundant kindness and mercy. We were lost, but he sought and found us; we were dead in trespass and sin, and he brought us back to life; we were trapped in the prison of fear, yet he set us free; we were blind until he gave us sight; we were soiled, then he cleansed us; we were hungry and thirsty before he fed us and gave us drink. This morning we thank you for these past forty days of Lenten reflection, and for the way that we have felt your everlasting arms bearing us up throughout them all. We rejoice in this table of meeting where we can share the cup in remembrance of him, and receive redemption through his blood and the riches of his grace lavished on us. Amen.

Biblical Allusions—John 1:16; Luke 15; Ephesians 2:1;
Deuteronomy 33:27

COMMUNION PRAYERS FOR HOLY WEEK
Palm/Passion Sunday

For the Bread

O God, this morning we see you coming to save us in Jesus Christ riding on the back of a colt. And with the gathered crowd we cry out "Hosanna," "Please Lord, save us now!" Save us from sin, darkness, and death. Save us from guilt and shame. Save us from our enemies and ourselves. Save us from discouragement and despair. Save us from settling for easy answers and from thinking that there are no answers. In the breaking of the bread here at your table this morning, we remember Christ's engagement with everything that threatens to undo us, and we are thankful and emboldened by your Spirit to keep moving down the road of your saving purposes for us and the whole world in him. Amen.

Biblical Allusions—Matthew 21:1–10; 1 John 3:8;
Hebrews 2:14–15; Matthew 12:29

For the Cup

Saving God, what we could not do for ourselves, you have done for us by sending Jesus Christ to deal with sin. Set free from its powerful hold on us, we are now free to walk according to the Spirit in the ways of life and peace. On this Sunday morning when we remember Christ's triumphal entry into Jerusalem to begin his journey to the cross, remind us that he walked this path for us. As we share the cup of the new covenant made possible in his blood, fill us this morning with sorrow for our sins and joy for Christ's willing obedience that led him to Calvary. Amen.

Biblical Allusion—Romans 8:1–8

Maundy Thursday

For the Bread

This is the night of mandates, Commanding God. Speak each one of them again directly to our hearts: to be foot–washing servants, to love as we have been loved, to break bread in remembrance of Christ's body given for us, and to receive the gift of the indwelling Spirit so that we might never feel abandoned or alone. Keep our obedience to your commands more than just ceremonial. As we break the bread in remembrance of Christ's sacrifice and in obedience to Christ's command in the upper room, send your Spirit to prod and push us into the deeper obedience of love and good works, we pray in the name of him who loves us more than we can imagine or deserve, Jesus Christ. Amen.

Biblical Allusions—John 13—16; Psalm 51:16–17;
Mark 14:22–25; Hebrews 10:24

For the Cup

In the sharing of this cup here tonight, God of yesterday, today, and tomorrow, take us back to that upper room in Jerusalem, where the cup was first shared by Christ with his disciples. Connect our confusion with theirs, our fear with theirs, our hope with theirs, and our trust with theirs. Assure us by the Spirit that you are just as present here as you were there; and just as everything converged for them at the cross, so may everything for us now spring from that cross. Saved by the sacrificial love of Calvary, now help us to live lives of sacrificial love ourselves because of Calvary, we pray in Christ's name. Amen.

Good Friday

For the Bread

Suffering God, on this day of the cross let us draw near enough to hear the voice of your Son, our Savior, saying, "Father, forgive them." This day contains mysteries that we will never fully understand. But this much is clear: Jesus Christ is on that cross for us. This is about forgiveness. Christ died for our sins. Our broken lives, his broken body, your broken heart, and this broken bread are all related. Through the Holy Spirit make our time here at your table today more than just a recollection of history. Indeed, make it the very foundation of our living, here and in the world to come. Amen.

Biblical Allusions—Luke 23:34; 1 Corinthians 15:3

For the Cup

On the cross Jesus Christ said, "I am thirsty," Holy and Merciful God. And so are we. He was thirsty from the suffering that he had endured and the sacrifice that he had embraced; and we are thirsty for the grace that his suffering and sacrifice supplies. As we come to this table on the day of the cross to share the cup of remembrance once again, may your Spirit remind us of how Jesus said that "those who eat my flesh and drink my blood have eternal life, and I will raise them up on the last day; for my flesh is true food and my blood is true drink," and give us understanding. Show us how to abide in you, and you in us, we pray. Amen.

Biblical Allusions—John 19:28; 16:12–15; 6:54–56

Holy Saturday

For the Bread

God of Promise and Presence, on this day of silence between the struggle of Good Friday and the victory of Easter Sunday, show us how to wait patiently with expectation. Because we live our lives of faith right here, in-between the already and the not yet, teach us how to trust you for what has been promised but has not yet come to pass. At this table where we break the bread of remembrance, supply us this day with the substance of things hoped for and provide us with the evidence of things not seen. And by the quickening of your Spirit within, guarantee to us the fulfillment of the promises for which we long, we pray. Amen.

Biblical Allusions—Hebrews 11:1; Romans 8:24–25;
2 Corinthians 1:22; Ephesians 1:13

For the Cup

In hope we are saved, Trustworthy God. But we hope for what we do not see, and that isn't always easy for us to do. So many times in our lives it looks like evil will prevail, and so many times in our world it looks like death gets the final word. So teach us the power of the patience of faith that Holy Saturday speaks. It's the grain of wheat that falls into the earth and dies that bears much fruit. Keep us trusting for that harvest of life, abundant and eternal. Nourish our hope by this cup of remembrance of Christ's blood shed, and pour into our hearts a fresh measure of the Holy Spirit so that we will cling to the hope in you that does not disappoint us. Amen.

Biblical Allusions—Romans 8:24–25; John 12:24; Romans 5:5

COMMUNION PRAYERS FOR EASTER
Easter Sunday

For the Bread

God of Power and Might who declared Jesus Christ to be your Son by raising him from the dead on the third day, we come to your table today to break the bread in remembrance of his dying and in hope of sharing his rising. Continue to put to death in us anything that is inconsistent with our identity as your beloved sons and daughters, and by the power of your life-giving Spirit raise us to walk in newness of life, we pray. Amen.

Biblical Allusions—Romans 1:4; 6:1–11

For the Cup

This cup that we raise at your table this morning, Resurrecting God, is not a toast to the memory of a long-lost friend, but an expression of our fellowship with a living companion. We thank you today not only that Jesus Christ died for our sins as our loving Savior, but that he was raised on the third day so that we might triumph over anything that would hold us back from walking in newness of life with him who is our living Lord. As this cup is the seal of the new covenant now established by Christ's blood, so let it also be the sign of our deliverance and transformation by the continuing work of your indwelling Spirit, in our hearts, we pray. Amen.

Biblical Allusions—1 Corinthians 10:16; Colossians 3:1–4

The First Sunday after Easter

For the Bread

Powerful God, by his resurrection from the dead you declared Jesus Christ to be your Son. We gather about his table here this morning to break bread because we have made him, his life, and his teachings, the very foundation of our lives. Upon that foundation we are now building with care, even as we are being built up into a spiritual house where acceptable sacrifices are offered to you. Make us a temple of your Holy Spirit, and accept our sacrifices of love and gratitude, we pray in Christ's name. Amen.

Biblical Allusions—Romans 1:4; Matthew 7:24–25;
1 Corinthians 3:11; 1 Peter 2:5

For the Cup

God of Light and Love, we have found your truth in Jesus Christ, and it has set us free. As we bless this cup in remembrance of Christ's blood poured out for us on Calvary's cross, enlighten us by your Spirit this morning to see again how he could not be defeated and how his message of reconciling love could not be silenced. Move us from the contest of Good Friday to the vindication of Easter Sunday, and help us to have the assurance of faith in our hearts and a confidence in your truth in our minds, focused on Jesus Christ who is the truth. Amen.

Biblical Allusions—John 8:32; Acts 2:24; 35;
Hebrews 6:4; Isaiah 62:3

The Second Sunday after Easter

For the Bread

Present and Abiding God, we gather at this table here this morning not just to remember something that happened a long time ago on a cross outside Jerusalem, but to affirm a present experience in our hearts. This broken bread is not merely a reminder of Jesus crucified; it's a sign of the risen Christ's presence. We have gathered at your table with such great expectations: the expectation that you will be in our midst; the expectation that we will meet you in the breaking of the bread; and the expectation that you will send the Holy Spirit afresh, that we might know your companionship and experience your presence with us always, we pray. Amen.

Biblical Allusions—Matthew 18:20; Luke 24:35; John 14:18

For the Cup

Living God, because of Jesus Christ, we call you "Emmanuel," the "God who is with us." In Jesus Christ you shared our flesh and blood so that you would understand what we go through each day. And then in Jesus Christ you shed your blood that we might be set free from everything that threatens to undo us. In blessing and drinking this cup here this morning, we are mindful and grateful for the blood that you shared with us and shed for us. Send your Spirit alongside to strengthen and sustain until that day when our faith becomes sight, we pray in Jesus' name. Amen.

Biblical Allusions—Matthew 1:23; Hebrews 2:14–18;
John 14:16; 2 Corinthians 5:7

The Third Sunday after Easter

For the Bread

O God, whose Kingdom will come, whose will shall be done on earth as it is heaven, open our eyes to be able to see in the jumble of the circumstances of this week the outline of your eternal purposes for us and our world. The cross of Jesus Christ brings into focus for us the way that you work to accomplish your saving intentions. In the breaking of this bread here this morning in remembrance of Christ's body broken for us, remind us once again of the patience of your sacrificial love and the power of your resurrection. Cultivate in us the fruit of patience and gentleness as evidence of your indwelling Spirit, as we work with you to change the world as well as ourselves, that all things might better reflect your desires and declare your glory, through Jesus Christ our Savior we pray. Amen.

Biblical Allusions—Matthew 6:10; Galatians 5:22–23;
Philippians 4:20

For the Cup

We are being changed, day by day, O God our Maker and Redeemer, through the death of Jesus Christ, which brings us the forgiveness of our sins, and through the resurrection of Jesus Christ, by which we are raised to walk in newness of life. As we share this cup of the new covenant from your table here this morning, fill us anew with the Holy Spirit that we might have the inward assurance that we are yours and see some external evidence that we are indeed becoming new creatures in Christ. Continue the work of salvation begun in us, and find us complete on the day of Jesus Christ, we pray. Amen.

Biblical Allusions—2 Corinthians 3:18; Romans 6:4;
Galatians 4:4–6; 2 Corinthians 5:17; Philippians 1:6;
Colossians 2:10; 1 Thessalonians 5:23

The Fourth Sunday after Easter

For the Bread

Parenting God, through the years this table has been a sacred gathering place for this part of your family. We have met here every Sunday morning to break the bread of remembrance of him whose sacrificial love has made us one. And the bond we have in your Spirit transcends time so that the memory of those we love but see no longer lingers here where we knew them as brothers and sisters who shared with us this journey of faith. As they sing your praise, and that of the Lamb slain from the foundation of the world, thin the gulf that divides us so that we might know that we are still one family by your saving love; here and there; now and always. Because you raised Jesus Christ from the dead, we know that even though we die, yet shall we live. In the blessed hope of that glorious promise of resurrection and life, we live today and long for tomorrow. Amen.

Biblical Allusions—Revelation 5:6–12; John 11:25

For the Cup

God of Feasts and Friends, your Son Jesus Christ ate and drank with sinners when he walked this earth. In fact, they called him a drunkard and a glutton because of the frequency of his table fellowship with them. And when the time came for Christ to do your will by becoming obedient unto death, even death upon a cross, he left this cup as the sign of his shed blood, and this table as a place of abiding fellowship with him. Here we receive the cup of forgiveness and share the wine of new life in him. And now we live and die in the promise that in heaven a banquet table is prepared with a space reserved for us, where we will sit with Christ forever in his fellowship. Here this morning, as we raise this cup in faith, pull tight the thread that links that past with this present, and this present with that future. In your Spirit let yesterday, today, and tomorrow dissolve into the eternity of your love in Jesus Christ that this cup represents, we pray. Amen.

Biblical Allusions—Luke 15:1–2; Matthew 11:19;
Philippians 2:8; 1 Corinthians 11:25; Revelation 19:6–9

The Fifth Sunday after Easter

For the Bread

Death remains our enemy; sin our problem; and shame our curse, O God of the cross and the tomb. We've accepted by faith the gospel of your Son Jesus Christ, and we have come to this table to break this bread here this morning as a way of renewing that commitment of our hearts and souls. But even as we come this morning, O God, we know that the gap between what we believe you have done for us in Jesus Christ and who we are becoming in Jesus Christ is still scandalously wide. For every step forward, it feels like we fall two back. The old person we were still haunts us, and the new person we are becoming is slow to develop. So this morning through the breaking of this bread reassure us that there is no condemnation for those who are in Christ Jesus, and send your Spirit in fresh measure that we might know that we are indeed your daughters and sons, and find the strength to keep growing in that identity, we pray in the name of Jesus Christ who is our Savior, Amen.

Biblical Allusions—1 Corinthians 15:56;
Romans 7:15–24; 8:1; 8:14–16

For the Cup

The journey from the first stirrings of our faith until that day we are finally face to face with you, O Saving God, is long and hard. We have seasons of growth and seasons of stagnation; days when we know that you are there and days when we can find no visible trace of your presence. The constant is this table with its bread and cup. It's here when we feel your grace just as it's here when we feel that we are just barely hanging on. Today as we drink from this cup of remembrance, which is the emblem of Christ's life blood poured out for us, teach us that you are there and will be faithful regardless of what we feel. Refresh the seal of your Spirit on us, which marks us as your own, and continue to move us along our journey of faith until we arrive safely at home. Amen.

Biblical Allusions—1 Corinthians 13:12; James 1:17;
2 Corinthians 1:21–22

The Sixth Sunday after Easter

For the Bread

The trappings of Easter have faded, O God of the Garden Tomb. The lilies are gone from the sanctuary; the hymns of resurrection have all been sung though; the stories of Christ surprising his friends by showing up with proofs that he is alive have all been told; the banners and posters of hope and new life are about to come down and be put away. The Easter season is coming to an end for another year; just don't let us make the mistake of putting away our Easter faith along with all those decorations. At this table where each week we break the bread in remembrance of how Christ died, stir us to remember that he was raised and is now alive. Open the eyes of our hearts by your indwelling Spirit so that we can know the risen Christ and make him known. Let this and every Sunday be a little Easter for us, we pray, in the name of Jesus Christ our risen Lord and constant companion. Amen.

For the Cup

Here at this table where we remember how Jesus Christ shed his blood for us and our redemption, Loving God, remind us that we do not serve a dead Savior but a living Lord. You raised Jesus Christ from the dead, and he is alive forevermore. We believe that with our heads; now help us to experience it more fully in our hearts. Make our weekly communion more than just a recollection of sacred history long past, but by your enlivening Spirit, speak and act in unmistakable ways in our lives so that we can know the reality of Easter year round, and not just at Eastertide, we pray in the name of him who lives in us today. Amen.

Ascension Day

For the Bread

Invisible and Immortal God, although no longer visible to our eyes, your Son promised that we would not be left as orphans when he took his leave. He assured us of his abiding presence with us in the breaking of the bread when we gathered in his name, and he promised that he would send another counselor to us, the comforter and helper who would continue to abide in us. And so today we claim with thanksgiving every sign of his presence in us, and with us. In the breaking of the bread and the Spirit's abiding in our hearts, we rejoice in Christ's constant companionship. May we ever abide in him, and him in us, we pray. Amen.

Biblical Allusions—John 14:15, 18; Matthew 18:20;
John 14:15

For the Cup

Present God, although we do not see Jesus Christ right now, still we love him; and even though we were not with Jesus Christ when he dwelt among humanity and they beheld his glory, yet we believe in him and rejoice in the salvation of our souls through him. What we have is the witness of the Word, the assurance of the Holy Spirit, and the emblems of the gospel, such as this cup from which we drink here today. Until that day when our faith becomes sight, give us confidence in unseen realities and reassurance in promises yet to be fulfilled, we pray in Jesus' name. Amen.

Biblical Allusions—1 Peter 1:8–9; 2 Corinthians 5:7;
Hebrews 11:27

Pentectost Sunday

For the Bread

Today we thank you for fulfilling your promise, Faithful God, about pouring out your Spirit upon all your people. New hearts you have indeed given to us. A new Spirit you have indeed put inside us. A new covenant you have indeed established between us. A new way of knowing you and relating to you has indeed been provided for us by you. And so at this table where we break the bread in remembrance of Jesus Christ this morning, we celebrate our renewal and offer you our thanks. Continue to keep us full of the Spirit that we might be empowered as your witnesses, we pray in Jesus name, the one who baptizes us in the Holy Spirit. Amen.

Biblical Allusions—Acts 2:17ff; Ezekiel 36:26–32;
Jeremiah 311- 34; Acts 1:8; Luke 3:16

For the Cup

We are your people, O God, created by your Word and Spirit. On this the birthday of the church, we celebrate your presence that calls us into being and sustains our life. In blessing and sharing this cup here today we are naming Jesus Christ as our Lord once again and are calling on the Holy Spirit to direct us in all of our ways. Confirm what is correct in us, and reform what is amiss. Make us channels through which your presence and power flow out into the world, rather than reservoirs that try to contain it for ourselves. And continue the saving work that you've already begun in us so that we might be used by you in the salvation of the world, which we know to be your perfect will in Jesus Christ. Amen.

Biblical Allusions—Philippians 1:6; 2:12–13;
1 Timothy 2:4; 2 Peter 3:9

5

Communion Prayers for Special Sundays

Christians live in two worlds simultaneously. We are citizens of heaven (Phil. 3:20) with a sworn allegiance to the kingdom of God, and we are residents of this world with important responsibilities to, and a genuine affection for, a particular place and time. Juggling the demands of Christ and culture can be tricky, especially in worship. What do you do on the Sunday when Mother's Day and Pentecost coincide? Some Christians have concluded that the world and its special days have no place in the sanctuary of God. Other Christians mark the holidays of the secular calendar on Sunday mornings with no qualms of conscience whatsoever. And many Christians wrestle with the competing claims every time the ways of Christ and Caesar intersect.

What you choose to do on these special days at the Lord's table during the communion service is a matter of conscience, both individual and congregational. It is one of those "inferences" where our interpretations are going to vary; a "nonessential" where liberty and charity must prevail. As the spiritual leaders of a particular community of faith, we must be sensitive to the diversity of opinion that exists among our people, appreciative of the freedom that allows us to differ, and resolved to make sure that nothing becomes a "scandal" for the gospel other than Jesus Christ and Him crucified (1 Cor. 1:23). The communion prayers that you find in this section correspond to the Special Sundays for which worship materials appear in *Chalice Worship* (155–192).

The New Year

For the Bread

God of new beginnings, we live our lives between yesterday and tomorrow, between forgiveness and hope. On the threshold of this New Year we need your mercy for the failings of the past and the assurance of your companionship for the unseen and uncertain future. As we break the bread this morning that serves as the tangible reminder of the depth of your commitment to us in Jesus Christ, speak to us anew of the way that your love never lets us go. In the sure embrace of your Spirit, help us to forget what lies behind and to press on without fear to what lies ahead, we pray. Amen.

Biblical Allusion—Philippians 3:13

For the Cup

God of promise for tomorrow, the remembrance of your tender mercies in the past gives us such confidence for today and hope for tomorrow. This cup that we bless is the emblem of Christ's blood shed so freely for us and for all on Calvary's cross. As we drink of it this morning, bring to mind and heart other mornings at this table when in various circumstances your grace proved sufficient for our need at the moment. At the beginning of this New Year may we experience the peace that passes understanding, the work of your Spirit within us, we pray. Amen.

Biblical Allusions—2 Corinthians 12:9; Philippians 4:7

Week of Prayer for Christian Unity

For the Bread

Here at your table this morning, O God who judges the heart, help us to rightly discern the body. We break this bread to help us remember how your Son was crucified for us. We know how we are made whole by his brokenness. But we don't always see with that same clarity how this table has become a barrier rather than a bridge among your people, or how this broken bread is the sign of the brokenness of your other body, the church. Help us to confess the sin of disunity that sends us comfortably to separate tables, and then open our hearts to a new move of your Spirit so that we might rediscover the gift of unity that's already ours because Jesus Christ is our common Lord and only Savior. Amen.

Biblical Allusions—1 Corinthians 11:27–32; Ephesians 4:3

For the Cup

Blessing and sharing this cup here today, Gracious God, is a reminder of the sacrifice that your Son made so freely for us all. Christ made no distinctions between us in his dying. In fact, it was by the blood of Jesus that those who were far off and those who were close by were brought together and made into one new people. We have been reconciled into one body by the cross. So as we drink in remembrance of him this morning, remind us of our reconciliation and unity. In our access to you through him in the one Spirit, convict us of the sin of leaving anybody out, or anybody behind. By this cup and what it represents, preach peace to us, we pray. Amen.

Biblical Allusions—Acts 10:34; Ephesians 2:13–18

Week of Compassion

For the Bread

As we break this bread and freely share it here in your sanctuary this morning, O God of the poor and the powerful, we know that people just down the street and all around the world will taste no bread this day. As we celebrate your abundance, we are mindful of those who know little but deprivation and despair. In our gratitude for what you have provided for us here, may your Spirit unsettle us until all sit at table with us and share in the bounty of your grace in both creation and redemption, we pray. Amen.

Biblical Allusions—Psalm 146:8–10; 1 John 3:17–18

For the Cup

Living and Abiding God, we experience your presence in this cup of memory that we share here at the table today. It is a participation in the blood of Christ. And we experience your presence in the cool cups of water that are shared with the thirsty in your name. Keep these cups of your presence together in our hearts. May the world and its needs break constantly into our sanctuaries to disturb our complacency. And constructively send us from our sanctuaries back into the world to witness and serve, inspired by the sacrifice of your Son and empowered by your agitating Spirit. Amen.

Biblical Allusions—1 Corinthians 10:16; Matthew 10:42

Celebrations Honoring Scouting

For the Bread

God of Growth, we do not know much about the childhood or adolescence of Jesus Christ your Son. All of those years with their experiences and lessons get summarized for us in the simple words of the familiar Biblical phrase, "And Jesus increased in wisdom and in years, and in divine and human favor." Here at this table this morning, we break the bread in remembrance of what Jesus Christ did for us when he was fully grown, how in the intersection of the beams of Calvary's cross he fulfilled his mission of expressing love so that we might experience that divine and human favor in its fullness. Bless every human effort and association that teaches boys and girls to love God with all their hearts, souls, minds, and strength, and to love their neighbors as themselves. Send your enabling Spirit to all young people so that just like Jesus they will grow in wisdom and years, and in divine and human favor, we pray. Amen.

Biblical Allusions—Luke 2:52; Matthew 22:37–39

For the Cup

In the temple when he was just twelve years old, God of us all, your Son, Jesus Christ, amazed the teachers of the law with his understanding of you and your ways. In the days of his public ministry, God of us all, your Son, Jesus Christ, called for the children to come to him, for to such belongs the kingdom of God. And in the life of Christ's other body, the church, the command was spoken not to despise the youth, but to let them set the rest of us an example in speech and conduct, in love, in faith, and in purity. Today as we bless this cup in remembrance of what Jesus Christ did and said, turn the hearts of adults to children and youth, and the hearts of children and youth to adults. In the power of your Spirit help us to be a community in which children and youth are welcomed, and are given the discipline and instruction of the Lord, we pray. Amen.

Biblical Allusions—Luke 2:41–51; Luke 18:15–17;
1 Timothy 4:11–12; Malachi 4:5; Ephesians 6:4

Stewardship Sunday

For the Bread

We are amazed to know, O Saving God, that you have made us stewards of your grace, placing part of your eternal purpose in our frail hands, working with us and through us to complete the work of redemption begun for us in Christ Jesus our Lord. We offer ourselves here to be your faithful servants, your co-laborers, in the field that you are planting and the building that you are erecting. This morning as we break the bread in remembrance of his offering of himself for us—full, sufficient, and free—send your Spirit to break open our lives so that nothing is held back, but that everything is made available to you and your Kingdom through Jesus Christ our Lord. Amen.

Biblical Allusions—1 Corinthians 3:9; 4:1–2

For the Cup

We love because you first loved us. We forgive because we have been forgiven. We give because we have received. And we serve because we have been served. O God, this morning in the sharing of this cup we remember the primacy of Christ's self-giving love, how He emptied Himself and became obedient unto death, even death on a cross. As that death saves us, may it also now shape us. In the sharing of your Spirit, inspire us to do nothing from selfishness, but to look always to the interests of others before our own. Teach us the greater blessing of giving than receiving, and thereby help us to conform more closely to the image of your Son, our Savior, Jesus Christ. Amen.

Biblical Allusions—1 John 4:19; Philippians 2:1–8;
Acts 20:35; Romans 8:29

Earth Stewardship Sunday

For the Bread

Creator God, the bread we break comes from the fields that grow, and the saving sacrifice of Jesus Christ that this broken bread brings to mind and heart holds promise, not just for us, but also for all of creation. As we groan for our final redemption, so does the natural world. As we are even now becoming new creatures, show us how to live in anticipation of the new heavens and the new earth where the balance of shalom shall prevail again just as it did in the garden. As your Spirit brooded over the face of the deep in first creation, so send your Spirit now to brood over the face of your new creation, the church, filling us with wonder, responsibility, and praise, we pray. Amen.

Biblical Allusions—Romans 8:18–25; Isaiah 65:17–23;
Revelation 21:1; Genesis 1:2

For the Cup

Generously Giving God, without waiting for us to ask or demanding our thanks in return, you have provided for our physical well-being in abundance. From your generosity and goodness you have bestowed the gifts of creation: the changing seasons, the bounty of nature; the freshening rains; the energizing sun; the careful balance of the elements; the beauty of the sunset; and the amazing order of our very own bodies. Not only do we take such gifts for granted, too often we have been guilty of neglecting and abusing them, denying the stewardship we were created by you to exercise. So here at this table, where we are stewards of the mysteries of your gifts of redemption, we come seeking both forgiveness and restoration. In blessing this cup and by drinking it in faith here this morning, we seek the healing of everything our sin has broken. Heal the divisions in our relationship with you, in our relationship with ourselves, in our relationships with each other, and in our relationship with all of creation. Send your Holy Spirit, and so renew the face of the earth, together with us, we pray. Amen.

Biblical Allusions—Genesis 1:28–30; 1 Corinthians 4:1

Mother's Day

For the Bread

Strong, Gentle God, you have loved us like a mother. You have brought us forth, and we bear your image; the reflection of your heart. You have fed us from yourself and taught us how to walk in your ways. When we have strayed, your love has followed us. Just like a mother hen you have gathered us safely under your wings again and again. Here at this table this morning where we break the bread that connects us with the death of Jesus Christ on Calvary's cross, we are staggered once again by the thought of the sacrifice of your love. Insofar as we have experienced that same kind of love in our relationships with our earthly mothers, we thank you today. Insofar as we have not, we hold before you our desperate need, and pray that your Spirit will now enter our hearts and fill the empty places with the kind of love that bears all things, that believes all things, that hopes all things, that endures all things, that never ends—the kind of love you show us in Jesus Christ. Amen.

Biblical Allusions—Isaiah 66:13; Genesis 1:27; Hosea 11:1–8;
Luke 13:34; 1 Corinthians 13:6–8

For the Cup

Tenacious God, just as a mother cannot forget her nursing child, nor fail to show compassion to the children of her womb, so you have not forgotten us, nor failed to show us your compassion. We have presumed upon your loving kindness; we have taken advantage of your steadfast love, so that you would be more than justified in turning your back on us and walking way. But the heart has a logic of its own. Here at this table, sharing this cup, we taste and see just how good and gracious you really are. On the cross, Christ's life was poured out in love for us, and now, by your Holy Spirit, that love is poured into our hearts, filling us with endurance, character, and hope. Hold us firmly in your loving embrace as we cling in faith to you through Jesus Christ our Lord. Amen.

Biblical Allusions—Isaiah 49:15;
Romans 2:4, 5:5; Psalm 34:8

Christian Family Week

For the Bread

This morning we bow our knees to you, O God from whom every family in heaven and on earth takes its name. As we gather about this dinner table this morning to break the bread in remembrance of the sacrifice of our elder brother, Jesus the Christ, turn our hearts to one another in family love. Help us to relate to the older men as fathers and the older women as mothers; to the younger men as brothers and the younger women as sisters. Strengthen the bond of your Spirit within this household of faith so that our love for one another will bear witness to the world that your family always has room for more through Jesus Christ our Lord. Amen.

Biblical Allusions—Ephesians 3:14; Hebrews 2:11–12; Malachi 4:6; 1 Timothy 5:1–2; Ephesians 2:9; John 13:33–35

For the Cup

Giving and Forgiving God, at this table each week we remember how Jesus Christ, by taking up the cross, gave himself up for us all. This cup that we share in remembrance of his blood that was shed is our weekly reminder of the true cost of your love. So send us your Spirit in this time of communion that we might have the mind of Christ. Then as fathers and mothers, sons and daughters, people related to one another by the blood of family ties, and by the blood of Christ poured out, make us eager to be of the same mind, having the same love, and being in full accord. Sharing the Spirit of Christ through this communion service and in communion of this community of faith, make us humble so that we can live in harmony with one another, and willing so that we can attend to each other's needs, just as Christ on Calvary was humble and willing for us. Amen.

Biblical Allusions—Ephesians 5:25; 1 Corinthians 2:14–16; Philippians 2:1–4

Memorial Day

For the Bread

The greatest love is to lay down your life for your friends. So your Son taught us, O God of this Greater Love. Then to prove it, he laid down his life for us. Our sharing in this weekly remembrance of his sacrifice makes us mindful of the sacrifices to which we are called. Today we are especially mindful of all those who have given the full measure of devotion in laying down their lives for us in the protection of our liberties and the preservation of our national life. As we would dare not approach the table of the remembrance of the sacrifice of Christ Jesus in an unmindful, or ungrateful manner, so let us not go through this Memorial Day holiday unmindful of or ungrateful for the sacrifices that have been made by our brothers and sisters through the years. In our affirmation of this "no greater love" here this morning, teach us again that it is not finally by might, and not finally by power, but finally by your Spirit that your Kingdom comes. Amen.

Biblical Allusions—John 15:12–14; 1 Corinthians 11:27ff;
Zechariah 4:6

For the Cup

Beckoning God, the cup from which Jesus Christ asked to be released from drinking is the very cup we bless and share in remembrance of him. It is the cup of suffering, sacrifice, and redemption through his blood. In the days of his earthly pilgrimage, Jesus asked his friends if they were prepared to drink the cup that he would drink, and they said that they were able. Their lives were then poured out as offerings of thanksgiving to you. Today we are mindful of all whose lives have been poured out as cups of sacrifice and service. Fill us with the Spirit of that same kind of courage, and then send us out to give ourselves away after the example of Jesus Christ our Savior on the cross, and in the footsteps of all those who have taken up their own crosses and followed him. Amen.

Biblical Allusions—Luke 22:42; Matthew 20:23;
2 Timothy 4:6; Matthew 16:24

Father's Day

For the Bread

Strong, Sustaining God, you have loved us like a father. You have provided for our needs and protected us from our enemies. In Jesus Christ you took on sin and death and made available to us forgiveness and life, abundant and eternal. This broken bread is the emblem of his broken body for us. As we partake of it in faith here this morning, fill us anew with your Spirit so that our great desire will be to please you in all that we are and do. We want to live lives of gratitude, maturity, and responsibility, so direct our feet onto the paths of righteousness, and correct us when we go astray in our attitudes or our actions. Send us into the world, serving your purpose, relying on your power, knowing and making known your presence in Jesus Christ in whose name we pray. Amen.

Biblical Allusions—Psalm 23; John 10:11–18;
1 Corinthians 15:25–26

For the Cup

You told us to honor our earthly fathers, Commanding God, and we have tried to be faithful to this promise-filled instruction. Through our obedience we have learned what it means to be in relationship with you. Our parents were our first and best teachers of you. By their faithfulness, we learned about your faithfulness. By their authority, we learned about your authority. By their desire for our best, we learned about your desire for our best. And by their frailty and failures, we learned about the sufficiency of your grace. Jesus Christ our Savior wrestled with obedience to your will, and by drinking the cup of suffering on Calvary, he became the source of eternal salvation for all who now obey him. Today as we thankfully share this cup in remembrance of Christ's sacrifice, stir us up by your Spirit to an obedience in faith to all that has been commanded, and thus may we abide in your love and joy, we pray in the name of Jesus Christ, your Son. Amen.

Biblical Allusions—Exodus 20:12; Hebrews 5:7–9;
Romans 16:26; John 15:10–11

Independence Day

For the Bread

For freedom Christ has set us free, Liberating God, so help us now to stand firm in it, not submitting again to the yoke of slavery or using it to justify acts of selfish irresponsibility. Our bondage to self, rebellion, and death was crucified with Jesus Christ on Calvary's cross so that we could be set free to live in obedience to you. Today as we break this bread in remembrance of how and why Christ died, bring to our awareness the way that, in him, we have indeed died to self, been set free from sin, and are liberated for new possibilities. As we have no hope of succeeding in any of this by our own strength, empower us by your indwelling Spirit to enable us to walk in the freedom to which we have been called. As freedom is part of your purpose for us all, let us gladly affirm it, gratefully enjoy it, and diligently seek it in every sphere of life, we pray. Amen.

Biblical Allusions—Galatians 5:1, 13;
Romans 6:1–14; 8:1–11

For the Cup

Today we celebrate the freedom we enjoy as citizens, O God of All the Nations. We claim liberty and justice for all as part of our noble identity as a nation "under God." As citizens of heaven, we understand just how costly justice is and just how demanding liberty can be. In the way that your holiness and mercy contended on Calvary's cross, we see the absolute worth of justice, and in the pull we experience between flesh and Spirit in the crucified life, we know the challenge of freedom. We share this cup here this morning in remembrance of where the just requirements of the Law were satisfied and how we were set free from everything that held us in spiritual bondage. As part of our grateful response for what you have provided us through the death, burial, and resurrection of Jesus Christ, we renew our commitment to justice and liberty as part of your good purpose for all. Amen.

Biblical Allusions—Philippians 3:20; 1 John 2:2;
Galatians 5:17

Labor Day

For the Bread

God, you are a worker. In the work of creation you made a world of beauty and order, utility and delight. You made us in your image, after your likeness, and you placed us in the world to tend it as good stewards. When the rebellion of our sin spoiled everything that you had made with such skill and care, you began the work of redemption that climaxed on a Roman cross and in an empty tomb. The bread on your table is a gift from your work of creation, and what we now do with it—taking it, blessing it, breaking it, and eating it—points to the gift of your work in redemption through Jesus Christ. We are thankful for all the works of your hands that we experience here this morning, Creating and Redeeming God. Now, restored by the love of your Son and renewed in the power of your Spirit, we are ready to be your coworkers as was your intention in the beginning, and has now been made possible again through Jesus Christ our Lord. Amen.

Biblical Allusions—Genesis 1—2; 1 Corinthians 3:9

For the Cup

In the heat of the day and the strain of the toil, Sabbath God, you invite us to stop for a deep breath and a refreshing drink. We know the gift that rest is to our physical bodies. We were made by you to live active lives and have meaningful work, but not ceaselessly. The Sabbath was made for us; rest is one of your good gifts. So spiritually you call us to Sabbath at this table each week. "Come to me, all of you that are weary and are carrying heavy burdens," was your Son's invitation; "and I will give you rest" was his promise. "Drink from the well of eternal life," was his invitation; "and you will never thirst again" was his promise. Your Spirit says, "Come…let everyone who is thirsty come… and drink in the gift of life." And so we do, with grateful hearts and rested souls. Amen.

Biblical Allusions—Genesis 2:1–3; Mark 2:27; Matthew 11:28;
John 4:13–14; Revelation 22:17; Hebrews 3:7—4:13

Reconciliation Sunday

For the Bread

We break one loaf here at your table today, O God, the Creator and Redeemer of us all, and we celebrate your love manifested so powerfully to all of us in Jesus Christ our Lord and Savior. Belonging to him, we know that there is no longer any distinction to be made between us on the basis of race, economics, social standing, or gender. We rejoice that we are all one in Jesus Christ. Now, by your Spirit inside each one of us, draw us closer to each other as the best evidence that we have been grasped by your inclusive love in Jesus Christ, our common Lord and Savior. Amen.

Biblical Allusion—Galatians 3:28

For the Cup

Reconciling God, when your church was reluctant to step across the walls of suspicion and prejudice, you sent your Spirit in fullness on those outside so that those inside would know your heart's desire to reconcile all things to yourself, making peace through the blood of Christ's cross. This morning as we share this cup in celebration of the redemption that is ours through Christ's blood, the experience of the forgiveness of our sins and the riches of your mercy, we pray that the witness of your Spirit may be heard clearly in the church again that you are a God who shows no partiality, but that all who come by faith are welcome, because of Jesus Christ who is our peace. Amen.

Biblical Allusions—Acts 10:34–48; Ephesians 1:7–10;
Colossians 1:20

World Communion Sunday

For the Bread

Enlarge our vision of your church this morning, O God of us all. As we surround this table here to break bread in remembrance of how Christ was given for us, let us catch a glimpse of other Christians in other places surrounding other tables breaking bread in remembrance of Christ given for them as well. By your Spirit link the hearts of all who this day draw near by faith to receive the emblems of Holy Communion with thanksgiving. Transcend national boundaries, denominational barriers, cultural differences, and ethnic divides so that as one people with one voice we confess our one faith in Jesus Christ our Lord, the Lamb who offers salvation to all. Amen.

Biblical Allusion—Revelation 7:9–10

For the Cup

Creator God, you made us from one blood. Redeemer God, you have saved us through the blood of One. Today at this table where we bless this cup and share it in remembrance of that blood shed for us all, convict us of any feelings of superiority or advantage that we might harbor. Remind us how, made and saved by you, we are all one. And claiming this as the most basic truth about us as your people, let our unity be the convincing proof of the claims of Jesus Christ to be the Lord and Savior of all, we pray. Amen.

Biblical Allusions—Acts 17:26; John 17:20–21

Heritage Sunday

For the Bread

Following where you lead, Beckoning God, requires spiritual courage. Today as we break this bread in remembrance of Christ's body given for all, we are mindful of the way that this table and its feast have not always been open to all. We are grateful for our Stone/Campbell legacy of breaking down the dividing walls of denomination so that anyone who believes in Jesus Christ might draw near by faith and receive these emblems of your saving love with thanksgiving. Because there is just one body, just one Spirit, just one hope, just one Lord, just one faith, just one baptism, and just one God, make us eager to maintain the unity of the Spirit in the bond of peace that is our special mission as a church. Amen.

Biblical Allusions—Ephesians 2:14; 4:1–5

For the Cup

Drinking from this cup of memory and blessing this morning, O God of our yesterday, our today, and our tomorrow, we are grateful for the life, death, and resurrection of Jesus Christ whose love makes us your people, whose example shows us the way, and whose abiding Spirit keeps us going. We know that we are not the only Christians, but help us to be Christians only. With Christ as our creed and the Bible as our guide, teach us how to exercise liberty in the nonessentials, unity in the essentials, and experience charity in all things. Amen.

All Saints' Day

For the Bread

We run our race, O Beckoning God, surrounded by a great cloud of witnesses, fixing our eyes on Jesus, the author and perfecter of our faith. Grateful for the example and witness of those who have gone before us, this morning we come to your table to break the bread, mindful of the way that Jesus Christ endured the cross, despised the shame, and found the joy that was set before Him. Celebrating the joy that our unseen but still loved brothers and sisters have entered— through the gate to eternal life that is death—we pray for a foretaste of that same joy as a fruit of your Spirit here and now. Amen.

Biblical Allusions—Hebrews 12:1–2;
Matthew 25:21; Galatians 5:22

For the Cup

O God of Promises, today we cling to them all; but especially to the one about nothing ever being able to separate us from your love; to the one about traveling with us through the valley of the shadow of death; to the one about going to prepare a place and then coming back for us; and to the one about us living even though we die. Today at this table of your promised presence, where we bless the cup in remembrance of Jesus Christ, and him crucified, we thank you for the way that all of your promises find their "yes" in him. We ask for a fresh outpouring of your Spirit, that we might be people of confident hope and abiding trust. Amen.

Biblical Allusions—Romans 8; Psalm 23;
John 10, 14; 2 Corinthians 1:20

Thanksgiving Sunday

For the Bread

Generous God, we know that we are blessed to live in this free land and to partake of its rich abundance. This week we will gather at family dinner tables all over this great nation to partake of its bounty and to voice our thanks for your gracious provision. In the same way, we gather here at another family dinner table this morning in the sanctuary of your church to partake of the bounty of your grace and to voice our thanks for your generous provision in Jesus Christ. On Thursday give us grateful hearts for the wonderful privilege of being Americans. But this morning, on this Lord's Day, as we break the bread in remembrance of him who gave himself for us, and for all regardless of nationality, remind us by your Spirit living in our hearts of our higher allegiance to your Kingdom and of our truer identity as its citizens through Jesus Christ in whose name we pray. Amen.

Biblical Allusions—John 18:36; Philippians 3:20

For the Cup

Truly our cup overflows, God of Bounty. We live in a world of beauty and balance. We inhabit a nation of freedom and justice for all. We belong to families of love and support. We occupy bodies that are fearfully and wonderfully made. Everywhere we look we see ample evidence of your provision and care. But nowhere does your grace become better focused for us than at this table. Blessing this cup this morning we remember how you loved the world so much that you gave your only begotten Son. Drinking from this cup this morning in faith we receive again the gift of your light and life. Filled anew with your Spirit, we ask that you fill our hearts with thanksgiving and our mouths with praise. Amen.

Biblical Allusions—Psalm 23:5; Psalm 139:14; John 3:16

National Bible Week

For the Bread

Even as we eat this bread here at your table today, O God of abundant supply, we know that we do not live by bread alone, but by every word that proceeds from your mouth. There are famines of bread to which we compassionately respond, just as Jesus fed the hungry multitudes in his day. And it is good that we do. But today as we share this spiritual bread broken in remembrance of Christ and him crucified, remind us of another famine, not a famine of bread but a famine of hearing the words of the Lord. As Jesus broke and multiplied the loaves at hand to feed the hungry, so send your Spirit so that we can break and multiply the bread of life we hold in our hands to feed the spiritually starving, we pray in the name of him who is the Word, Jesus Christ. Amen.

Biblical Allusions—Matthew 4:4; Amos 8:11–14;
John 1:1, 6:1–14

For the Cup

"Jesus loves me! This I know, for the Bible tells me so." Speaking and Acting God, we've come to this table this morning and blessed this cup because we believe "that Christ died for our sins in accordance with the scriptures, and that He was buried, and that he was raised on the third day in accordance with the scriptures." Today as we thank you for this cup that represents to us the death, burial, and resurrection of Jesus Christ our Lord, we also want to thank you for the scriptures, which bear witness to those saving events. By the anointing of your Spirit, we enter into an understanding of the truth of your Word. So as we search the scriptures seeking eternal life, always bring us to Jesus, the living and abiding Word, we pray. Amen.

Biblical Allusions—1 Corinthians 15:3–4;
John 2:20–27, 5:39; 1 John 1:1

Hymn Allusion—"Jesus Loves Me"
—Chalice Hymnal no. 113 (v. 1)

AIDS Sunday

For the Bread

Coming to this table each week, Always Present God, provides us with a powerful experience of being with Jesus Christ. In the breaking of the bread our eyes are opened, and we see how you are really there. Being with you here in this hour helps us to recognize how you are present by your Spirit in other places and at other times. This week help us to see you especially in "the distress and disguise" of those who suffer from AIDS. Alert to your presence and aware of your love here at this table, we beg you to show us your presence and make us channels of your love in the lives of those who live in-between hope and fear, rejection and acceptance, life and death. We pray in the name of Christ who shares all of these experiences fully and freely with us. Amen.

Biblical Allusions—Luke 24:30–31; Matthew 25:34–40;
Hebrews 4:14–16

(The "distress and disguise" phrase is
attributable to Mother Teresa.)

For the Cup

The cup of sorrow that we share together at this table today, Always Caring God, directs us to the sufferings of your Son on Calvary's cross. His willing embrace of that cross, his full entry into that experience of suffering, assures us that wherever people suffer today, Christ is also present. If Christ is there, so need we be, too. In your Spirit, bind us together so that we will weep with those who weep, suffer with those who suffer, hope with those who hope, and rejoice with those who rejoice. Sharing this cup, we ask you to show us how to share our lives through him who loves us all, Jesus Christ our Lord. Amen.

Biblical Allusions—Matthew 25:34–40; Romans 12:15

Peace/Shalom Sunday

For the Bread

Giving God, among the gifts that we come to this table this morning to receive is the gift of peace. In the breaking of this bread we are affirming the precious truth that Jesus is our peace: in our relationship with you broken by sin, in our hearts familiar with fear, in our interpersonal relationships characterized by brokenness, and in our world torn with violent strife. Fill us with your Spirit as your children, and as your children make us peacemakers, we pray. Amen.

Biblical Allusions—Acts 10:31; Romans 5:1, 12:18;
Ephesians 2:15–17; Galatians 5:22;
Luke 2:14; Matthew 5:8

For the Cup

God of Peace, we drink from this cup at your table here this morning as a sign of the peace now made between us through the death of your Son, our Savior, Jesus Christ. Where our sin had created an insurmountable barrier between us, Christ came and broke down the dividing wall of hostility. Through the gift of your Spirit we now have peace, peace not as the world gives it, but the peace that issues from a reconciled and reconciling heart. Send us from this table this morning renewed in that Spirit of peace, and call us to the ministry of reconciliation—your ambassadors inviting others to be reconciled to you through the righteousness of Christ, we pray. Amen.

Biblical Allusions—Romans 5:1; Ephesians 2:14; John 14:27;
2 Corinthians 5:17–20

Mission Sunday

For the Bread

Sending God, you sent Christ; you and Christ sent the Spirit; and now the Spirit sends us. Forgive us for settling in and for settling down when still so much remains that you've sent us to do: to bring good news to the poor, to proclaim release to the captives, to provide the recovery of sight to the blind, to let the oppressed go free, and to proclaim the year of the Lord's favor. Here at this table this morning in the breaking of this bread, as we claim and celebrate every one of these blessings of our salvation provided by Jesus Christ—crucified, risen, and exalted—let us not be complacent or content until these very same blessings have been shared with everyone, everywhere. Amen.

Biblical Allusions—John 20:21–23; Luke 4:18–19

For the Cup

Thrice Holy God—Holy, Holy, Holy, Lord of hosts—our uncleanness makes us unworthy to be here in your presence. Have mercy on us. Blot out our sin, and burn away our guilt. Only by the exercise of your mercy in Jesus Christ our Savior dare we to approach your throne. In the sharing of this cup symbolic of the blood of Jesus poured out for us, assure us of the tear in the veil that has kept us away from you, and make us bold to enter where Christ has opened a way for us. Once we are there, speak to us the words of your commission: "Whom shall I send, and who will go for us?" Here we are, Lord, send us. But give us your Spirit as well, Lord, so that we do not go alone. Amen.

Biblical Allusions—Isaiah 6:1–8; Hebrews 10:19–22

6

Communion Prayers for
Special Occasions

In special moments in the lives of individuals and
congregations, the presence of Jesus Christ is especially
needed and welcomed in the sign of bread and cup. It is
important to remember at such times that it is never
appropriate to restrict participation in the Lord's supper as
an ordinance of the gospel and a means of grace to a select
few. When the bread is broken and the cup is blessed, it
should be offered to all who can draw near and receive it by
faith with thanksgiving. The mechanics of the full participation of the faithful in a communion service on such a special
occasion will have to be worked out in each particular setting,
but the question of the full participation of the faithful in the
communion service has already been settled by the gospel
itself. When Jesus Christ is lifted up, he draws all people to
himself (Jn. 12:32), and we are specifically forbidden by him
to restrict the access of any who might want to come to him
(Mk. 10:14).

At a Baptism

For the Bread

Regenerating God, for our new birth into a living hope through the resurrection of Jesus Christ from the dead, we give you thanks this day. With all who have been buried with Christ into his death and raised with Christ to walk in newness of life, we come to this table remembering his death, burial, and resurrection, and renewing our own experience of death to self, burial of the past, and resurrection to new possibilities. With this broken bread we mark our break with what has come before; and by the beckoning of your Spirit within, we press on to your upward call in Christ Jesus our Lord. Help us to better know him and the power of his resurrection, we pray. Amen.

Biblical Allusions—1 Peter 1:3; Romans 6:1–11;
Philippians 3:10, 12–14

For the Cup

Just as newborn infants long for the rich milk that nurtures their physical growth, O Nurturing God, so we long for the pure, spiritual milk that will help us to grow up into the fullness of salvation. At this table, in this cup, O Nourishing God, we find the spiritual drink that satisfies our souls and delights our hearts. We thank you for quenching our deepest thirst by pouring your love shown in Christ's death into our hearts through the Holy Spirit that has been given to us. We pray that by your Spirit's indwelling presence we would be springs gushing up to eternal life. Amen.

Biblical Allusions—1 Peter 2:2; 1 Corinthians 10:1–4;
Romans 5:5; John 4:13–14

At a Wedding

For the Bread

Loving God, we believe that you are always and everywhere present. For this we are grateful. But we also know that you are especially present in certain places and at certain times by your sure promises: where two or three have gathered in your name, and where bread is broken in remembrance of Christ's death. Here today we have gathered in your name to join this man and this woman together in the bond of holy matrimony, and now we break this bread in remembrance and thanksgiving for the love that was shown on Calvary's cross. So we pray that according to your promise you will be present in a special way, both here in this sacred moment, and always in this partnership of love and trust that we bless today. May the gift of your Spirit strengthen every commitment we make, and may your sacrificial love seen in Jesus Christ always be the standard of our own love, we pray. Amen.

Biblical Allusions—Psalm 139:7–12; Matthew 18:20;
1 Corinthians 10:16–17

For the Cup

As wine was blessed and gladness increased at that wedding in Cana of Galilee, so here again at this wedding today we bless a cup and pray for the increase of gladness among us. Covenant God, whose commitment to us was sealed by the blood of Christ shed, may this cup of the new covenant seal the commitment of love now made here today between this man and this woman. Teach us again the costliness of covenant love by the example of your Son and by the joy that comes from willingly giving ourselves up for one another. Empower us by your indwelling Spirit, and make us all capable of the greatest love: the selfless giving away of ourselves, we pray in the name of him who gave himself to us, Jesus Christ our Lord. Amen.

Biblical Allusions—John 2:1–11; 1 Corinthians 11:25;
Ephesians 5:25; John 15:12–13

At a Healing Service

For the Bread

We are broken, God of Wholeness, some of us in body, some of us in spirit, and some of us in mind. We come because we trust your promises that broken people will not be turned away from your love and care. At this table with its broken bread, O God, we hear your invitation to come and the assurance that you truly understand. Because of Jesus Christ we know that we have a God who is able to sympathize with our weaknesses. And by your Spirit we trust that even our stammering uncertain prayers are heard and answered. Heal us by the broken body of your Son, we pray. Amen.

Biblical Allusions—Psalm 51:17; Isaiah 42:3; Matthew 12:20; Hebrews 4:15–16; Romans 8:26–27

For the Cup

On the cross Christ poured out his life as an offering for us all, O Giving God, and by his stripes we believe that we can be healed. So we take this cup, which is the sign of his shed blood, and we drink it today in faith and hope. We want to be healed. We long to be made whole. To whom else can we turn? You alone have the words of eternal life. So send your Spirit in this moment to soothe, strengthen, and sustain us in the power of your Son, we pray. Amen.

Biblical Allusions—Matthew 26:28; Isaiah 53:4–5; 1 Peter 2:24; John 6:68

During Homebound Communion

For the Bread

Faithful God, your promise in Jesus Christ was that we would neither be forgotten nor forsaken. In these days of restriction, it is indeed reassuring to know that you are here and that you care. In the sign of this bread broken and shared we know that you understand our circumstance and that your companionship is something we can count on in the days ahead. By your Holy Spirit, the promised Comforter, be present in this moment of communion with your gifts of solace and strength. Then remain to support and sustain us with your love, we pray in Jesus' name. Amen.

Biblical Allusions—Matthew 28:20; John 14:15–18

For the Cup

This cup that we share in this moment, Accompanying God, is the sign of your great love for us, poured out abundantly in Jesus Christ. On the cross where he was crucified, Jesus Christ created community—entrusting the care of his mother to his friend, and the care of his friend to his mother. Do that same work here and now by your Spirit, we pray. Help us who share this moment of communion together become a vital link in that new community of mutual compassion and care, we pray in the name of him who shed his blood to make us members one of another. Amen.

Biblical Allusions—John 19:25–27; Romans 12:5

At an Ordination

For the Bread

At this table where we break and share this bread representative of Christ's body broken, O God, we are reminded of how Jesus Christ came not to be served but to serve, and to give his life as a ransom for many. The Good Shepherd laid down his life for the sheep, and we now belong to your flock because of his faithful and sacrificial love. As we have partaken of the benefits of Calvary, so now help us by your Spirit also to embrace the invitation of Calvary to take up our crosses and follow him on paths of service and in lives of loving sacrifice. As Christ has given us an example, help us now to follow in his steps, we pray. Amen.

Biblical Allusions—Matthew 20:28; John 10:11;
Matthew 16:24–25; 1 Peter 2:21

For the Cup

At this table where we bless and share this cup representative of Christ's blood shed, O God, we are reminded of how Jesus Christ told his disciples that they would have to drink from it as well. As we drink from it here today, may our obedience be more than just ceremonial. Stir up the gifts of your Spirit that empower us for ministry, and then send us to where you need us to be, to do what you need us to do. Fed at your table, led by your Spirit, "Lord, we are able." Amen.

Biblical Allusion – Matthew 20:20–23

Hymn Allusion—"'Are Ye Able,'" Said the Master"
—Chalice Hymnal no. 621

At the Installation of a Minister

For the Bread

Constant God, in all the changes that we go through in this life, only your love never fails and only your goodness never changes. There is never any shadow of turning with you. Your faithfulness to us endures forever, from generation to generation. Throughout this recent season of transition in the pastoral leadership of our church, this table has been spread each week; and we have been able to break the bread that is symbolic of Christ's body given for us. Here we have learned again how to trust your provision and care. Indeed, you have been our shepherd, and we have wanted for nothing more. Now as the winds of the Spirit have blown in a new direction and we have been blessed with a new pastor, let us not forget your faithfulness or begin to rely on anything less than your provision for us in Jesus Christ. Amen.

Biblical Allusions—James 1:17; Psalm 23:1;
1 Peter 5:1–5; Hebrews 13:20

For the Cup

God of Abundance, by your rich mercy our cup overflows. You are not stingy with your grace, reluctant with your love, or hesitant in your care. All of our needs have been lavishly satisfied by you. You pour your love into our hearts through the Holy Spirit, and the blood of Jesus Christ cleanses us from all sin. Every week at this table we share the cup of forgiveness, and it never runs dry. So, at the beginning of this new ministry here this morning, let us experience that fullness of your Spirit so that goodness and mercy may attend to all that we will attempt in your name and for your glory. Amen.

Biblical Allusions—Psalm 23; Romans 5:5; 1 John 1:7;
Colossians 3:17

At the Dedication of a Church

For the Bread

In the center of this building that we have built to your glory, Abiding God, stands a table of remembrance and thanksgiving. Here each week we will break the bread of communion and remember how Jesus Christ became the chief cornerstone of the spiritual community that is being built stone upon stone to offer spiritual sacrifices acceptable to you. As we break that bread here this morning and tell that story, may Jesus Christ—crucified, risen, and exalted—become the foundation upon which a temple of the Holy Spirit will arise. As Christ gets lifted up here, draw all people to yourself, we pray in his name. Amen.

Biblical Allusions—1 Peter 2:4–5; 1 Corinthians 3:11–16;
John 12:32

For the Cup

We know, Eternal and Infinite God, that you cannot be confined to buildings made with human hands. So all we ask this morning is that this building be one of the places where people can always come to find you when they are looking, and from which you will move out to seek and find people even before they start to look for you. Fill us and this place with your Spirit of grace and power. At this table where the cup of the New Covenant made possible in Christ's blood is blessed and offered to all each week, may you be known and loved by all even as you know and love all, we pray in Christ's name. Amen.

Biblical Allusions—Acts 7:48–50; 1 Kings 8:22–53

At a Funeral

For the Bread

It helps us to know that you are familiar with this pain that we feel here today, O God. As Jesus wept at the grave of a friend before restoring him to life, so now we weep even though we believe that though we die, yet shall we live. As we break this bread in remembrance of Christ's death, remind us that in just three days his tomb was empty and the world was full of his presence even as the hearts of his friends were full of joy. Send your Spirit into the emptiness of our hearts now, so that in due season we might know that same joy because of that same presence of the risen Christ in whose name we pray. Amen.

Biblical Allusions—John 11:35; 11:25–26

For the Cup

In the garden your Son begged for the cup of death to pass from him, O Saving God. It was dark, and he struggled with what was coming. This is a day of darkness and struggle for us as well. We live in the shadow of death, and we have faced its fury again in this painful loss. But in the upper room on that same night before he died, Jesus took a cup, and after blessing it, he gave it to his friends while speaking of forgiveness and eternity. As we take, bless, and drink from this cup here today, speak of those things again so that our hearts will not be troubled or afraid. Amen.

Biblical Allusions—Matthew 26:39; Psalm 23:4;
Hebrews 2:14–15; John 14:1

Conclusion: Scripting the Moment

My son is an aspiring actor. Texas, where we live, has an annual statewide high school drama contest called "One Act." An entire play must be presented in one forty-minute act. This year his school is doing Hamlet. Now, as you know, Hamlet ordinarily takes hours to perform. But the cast has the action and script whittled down to forty minutes, and not one second longer. And that's because if the play should ever exceed the time limit, it's automatically disqualified.

Now, as you can imagine, no time is wasted in moving the story of Hamlet along to its dramatic climax—the final death scene—when you've only got forty minutes. But enough of the story has to be told to establish both the characters' identities and the movement of the plot line; otherwise the action on the stage would be sheer nonsense. The script is lean, and the acting fast-paced enough to get the story told in the allotted time frame. But should it ever run long in competition, there is a well-rehearsed doomsday scenario.

The student stage manager keeps a stopwatch on the performance from her booth. She knows what marks need to be hit, and when, to bring the play in at forty minutes. She has the authority to start bringing down the stage lights with a minute to go as the signal to the cast to wind it up, and fast. The cast has been instructed that wherever they are in the play, should those lights dim, the actors on stage need to start dying where they stand in quick succession so that the sweet prince can be told "goodnight" and the curtains pulled on time. It hasn't happened yet, and I hope it never does.

You see, Hamlet in forty minutes is dizzying enough without needing Hamlet to keel over prematurely. Besides, the climactic scene just wouldn't make any sense if it wasn't set up sufficiently. The same thing is true of worship. Rabbi Lawrence Hoffman in his 1988 book *The Art of Public Prayer* (The Pastoral Press) wrote helpfully about how public worship that works—that is, public worship that evokes a sense of genuine encounter with the living God—must be scripted like a good play to move the actors and their audience to the climactic moment of the drama. The question is, what are the climactic moments of our worship?

If you were going to diagram the worship service of a typical congregation of the Christian Church (Disciples of Christ), it would look something like a camel with its two humps. We do not agree on the order of worship, what comes first; but we do agree on the content of worship, that in whatever order we follow, we do the same two things. The worship tradition of the Christian Church (Disciples of Christ) focuses on two moments: the Service of the Word and the Service of the Table. In each of these two moments in our worship service we cherish the expectation that we will have an encounter with God in Jesus Christ. We expect to hear from God in Jesus Christ in the Word and to be with God in Jesus Christ around the table.

"Church" for Disciples means communion and a sermon each week. But neither of these two acts in our worship stands alone. We "ramp up" to the Word each Sunday morning with readings, music, and prayers, just as we respond to the Word with invitations, offerings, and singing. The same thing is true of the table. We don't immediately tear into the bread and start downing the cup when we sit down at the Lord's table on Sunday mornings. Part of the biblical mandate not to eat the bread and drink the cup of the Lord in an unworthy manner (1 Cor. 11:27) gets lived out for us in community by how we approach the Lord's supper. A communion hymn, a communion meditation, the words of institution, the breaking of the bread, the pouring of the cup, and the communion prayers all combine at the Lord's table to signal to the gathered community that the climactic moment of their encounter with God in Jesus Christ through the signs of bread and wine has arrived. The stage has been set; the story has been told; the significance has been noted; the moment has come. The weekly communion prayers of the elders at the Lord's table are some of the key elements in the unfolding of this process. Prayer in Jesus' name is the bridge that we cross over into the presence of God. An elder's weekly communion prayer does this for his or her gathered community of faith. It helps to build the bridge of encounter between God and people at the Lord's table.

In the Episcopal Church of my childhood, an acolyte rang a little set of bells at critical junctures of the service of holy communion as a way of signaling to the people in the pews that a sacred action was taking place at the altar for them: bread was being consecrated as the sign of Christ's body given for them; wine was being blessed as the sign of Christ's blood poured out for them. The saving death of Jesus Christ on Calvary's cross was being recalled and its benefits were being offered to all who would draw near by faith and receive the emblems with thanksgiving. Those bells were rung in the communion service of the church of my childhood as a way of letting everyone know that the climactic moment had arrived: the table was set, the feast of salvation was spread, the time to eat and drink had come. The prayers of elders at the Lord's table in our spiritual tradition do the same thing. It's highly unlikely that anybody is going to ring some bells when you start to pray at the Lord's table. But if bells are ringing in your soul as you pray, then the significance of what you are doing as an elder at the Lord's table will be clear, the grace of God known in Jesus Christ will be honored, and the faith of your gathered community will be served. This is what elders do. Elders pray.

Appendix

"On Prayer"—Alexander Campbell

When our founder Alexander Campbell sensed the need for a wholesale improvement in the quality of public praying in the life of our churches, he urged the adoption of the Reformed tradition of "conceived prayer." The Reformed tradition said that prayer could be taught by "stocking our hearts and minds with the thoughts and phrases" of scripture (Tripp 106). So in his essay "On Prayer," published as part of the first edition of his *Psalms, Hymns and Spiritual Songs* hymnal (1828), and again in the *Millennial Harbinger* periodical (1831), Alexander Campbell catalogued the twenty-two biblical prayers and benedictions that he thought could teach us to pray more faithfully and effectively.

1. A Prayer of Abraham—Genesis 18:23–32
2. A Prayer of Moses—Exodus 32:11–13
3. A Prayer of David—2 Samuel 7:18–20
4. A Prayer of Solomon—1 Kings 8:23–53
5. A Prayer of Ezra—Ezra 9:6–15
6. A Prayer of Nehemiah—Nehemiah 1:5–11
7. A Prayer of the Levites—Nehemiah 9:5–33
8. A Prayer of Daniel—Daniel 9:4–19
9. A Prayer of Hezekiah—2 Kings 19:15–19
10. Another Prayer of Hezekiah—2 Kings 20:3
11. A Prayer of Habakkuk—Habakkuk 3:2
12. The Aaronic Benediction—Numbers 6:20–26
13. The Disciples' Prayer—Matthew 6:9–13
14. The Prayer of the Publican—Luke 18:13
15. The Prayer of our Lord—John 17
16. The Prayer of the 120 Disciples—Acts 1:24–25
17. The Prayer of the Jerusalem Church—Acts 4:24–30

Sources Cited

Campbell, Alexander. *The Christian System.* 1839. Reprint, Nashville: Gospel Advocate, 1970.

——. "On Prayer." *Millennial Harbinger* 2, no. 11 (November 7, 1831): 497–503.

Cartwright, Colbert S., and O.I. Cricket Harrison, editors. *Chalice Worship.* St. Louis: Chalice Press, 1997.

Crow, Paul A., Jr., and James O. Duke , editors. *The Church for Disciples of Christ: Seeking to be Truly Church Today.* St. Louis: Christian Board of Publication, 1998.

Hoffman, Lawrence A. *The Art of Public Prayer.* Washington D.C.: The Pastoral Press, 1988.

Marshall, Catherine. *A Spiritual Life: A Man Called Peter and The Prayers of Peter Marshall.* New York: Inspiration Press, 1996.

Merrick, Daniel B., editor. *Chalice Hymnal.* St. Louis: Chalice Press, 1995.

Toler, Thomas W. *The Elder at the Lord's Table.* St. Louis: The Bethany Press, 1954.

Tripp, Diane Karay. "Daily Prayer in the Reformed Tradition: An Initial Survey," *Studia Liturgica* 21, no. 1 (1991).

Watkins, Keith. *Celebrate with Thanksgiving.* St. Louis: Chalice Press, 1991.

——. *The Breaking of the Bread.* St. Louis: The Bethany Press, 1966.

——. *The Feast of Joy.* St. Louis: The Bethany Press, 1977.

Watts, Isaac. *A Guide to Prayer.* London: Printed for Emanuel Mathews at the Bible in Pater-Noster Row, 1730.

White, James F. *Introduction to Christian Worship.* Revised edition. Nashville: Abingdon Press, 1990.

——. *Protestant Worship.* Louisville: Westminster/John Knox Press, 1989.